New Directions for
Higher Education

Martin Kramer
EDITOR-IN-CHIEF

New Ways to Phase into Retirement: Options for Faculty and Institutions

David W. Leslie
Valerie Martin Conley
EDITORS

Number 132 • Winter 2005
Jossey-Bass
San Francisco

LB
2334
.N48
2006

NEW WAYS TO PHASE INTO RETIREMENT:
OPTIONS FOR FACULTY AND INSTITUTIONS
David W. Leslie, Valerie Martin Conley (eds.)
New Directions for Higher Education, no. 132
Martin Kramer, Editor-in-Chief

Microfilm copies of issues and articles are available in 16mm and 35mm,
as well as microfiche in 105mm, through University Microfilms Inc., 300
North Zeeb Road, Ann Arbor, Michigan 48106-1346.

NEW DIRECTIONS FOR HIGHER EDUCATION (ISSN 0271-0560, electronic ISSN
1536-0741) is part of The Jossey-Bass Higher and Adult Education Series
and is published quarterly by Wiley Subscription Services, Inc., A Wiley
Company, at Jossey-Bass, 989 Market Street, San Francisco, California
94103-1741. Periodicals Postage Paid at San Francisco, California, and at
additional mailing offices. POSTMASTER: Send address changes to New
Directions for Higher Education, Jossey-Bass, 989 Market Street, San
Francisco, California 94103-1741.

New Directions for Higher Education is indexed in Current Index to Journals in Education (ERIC); Higher Education Abstracts.

SUBSCRIPTIONS cost $80 for individuals and $180 for institutions, agencies,
and libraries. See ordering information page at end of journal.

EDITORIAL CORRESPONDENCE should be sent to the Editor-in-Chief,
Martin Kramer, 2807 Shasta Road, Berkeley, California 94708-2011.

Cover photograph © Digital Vision

www.josseybass.com

CONTENTS

EDITORS' NOTES

The work that prompted the chapters in this volume was sponsored by the Alfred P. Sloan Foundation. We are grateful to Kathleen Christensen of the foundation for suggesting that we look at phased retirement as a model for more flexible work and career options for faculty. The TIAA-CREF Institute has been supportive as well, providing forums for the work of Steven Allen and Robert Clark on the University of North Carolina's phased retirement program (see Chapter Four).

Sloan's principal interest lies in ensuring that the academic workplace accommodates a new generation of faculty that will almost inevitably be more female than any other in history. Women are increasingly attaining advanced academic and professional degrees. In 1940, women received 13 percent of the Ph.D.s awarded; by 2001, they were receiving nearly half (47 percent). Census data also show that both men and women marry three to four years later now than was the case in 1940, meaning (presumably) that childbearing and child rearing take place later too. The rate at which women in their mid- to late thirties have children is rising, while the rate at which younger women have children is falling, according to the U.S. Census. Although most work in the home still seems to fall to women, the rise in dual-career couples means that both spouses inevitably need more time and flexibility in jobs and careers to accommodate young children.

The foundation for faculty career progression, the AAUP Statement on Academic Freedom and Tenure (American Association of University Professors, 2004), was adopted in 1940, over sixty years ago, and is at least three or four generations removed from the young Ph.D.s now aspiring to faculty careers. In 1940, the vast majority of faculty were men, and both men and women were more likely to have been in conventional marriages characterized by women not in the workforce. Today it appears more likely that young couples delay marriage and children until after both complete their graduate work and enter careers than would have been the case in 1940. It is also far more likely that both men and women will be professionals in demanding, competitive jobs.

We began our work on phased retirement assuming that flexibility was increasingly important for faculty who had mostly assumed they would retire at a given age but suddenly faced a range of choices and decisions about when and how to retire. Phased retirement would give them a way to accommodate their uncertainties without forcing an all-or-nothing retirement. We also assumed that what we could learn about flexibility for late-career faculty might be transferable to the growing need for flexibility for

NEW DIRECTIONS FOR HIGHER EDUCATION, no. 132, Winter 2005 © Wiley Periodicals, Inc.
Published online in Wiley InterScience (www.interscience.wiley.com) • DOI: 10.1002/he.192

junior faculty. In the end, we think the evidence does argue for more flexibility at both ends of the career continuum, a topic we discuss in Chapter Six. However, we also see important differences between policies and practices that help some exit their careers and jobs, and policies and practices that help younger faculty invest in career success and job stability. We focus closely in this volume on phased retirement, an option that provides flexibility for faculty who intend to retire but may have good reason to do so gradually instead of all at once.

Chapter One by David Leslie emphasizes the fundamental shift in the faculty retirement process: with the abolition of any mandatory retirement age, professors are now faced with choosing among alternative ways to retire. Phased retirement is one of these options.

Chapter Two by Valerie Martin Conley explores the contemporary retirement patterns of college and university faculty. This chapter draws on the most recent (1998) comprehensive national survey (the National Study of Postsecondary Faculty) conducted by the National Center for Education Statistics. It begins with an overview of the central tendencies and variations in faculty retirement patterns in general. It then analyzes the data further to explore who elects to phase and why. Economic factors appear more influential in women's retirement decisions; career success (or lack of it) appears more influential in men's. These patterns are borne out in the decision to opt for phased retirement too. Marital status and gender appear to jointly affect how individuals choose to retire. The principal finding of Conley's analysis is that faculty of both genders tend to retire in their mid-sixties with or without incentives and options.

Chapter Three by Natasha Janson draws on data from over one hundred interviews conducted during the Sloan study of phased retirement policies and from a wide array of policies reviewed in the course of that study. She breaks a sample of policies down into their several elements, describing, for example, who is typically eligible to elect phased retirement and what kinds of work assignments and pay are offered. Issues and problems in implementing phased retirement policies are raised and discussed, and ways to ensure mutually beneficial outcomes for individuals, their departments, and the institution are considered.

Chapter Four by Steven Allen, Robert Clark, and Linda Ghent provides an in-depth case study of phased retirement in the University of North Carolina (UNC) system. The first part of the chapter provides a general assessment of the purpose and nature of phased retirement in higher education. It draws on a national survey conducted under the auspices of the AAUP and on the authors' own studies of the university's experience with a systemwide policy. They find that the UNC plan has encouraged some faculty to retire who might not have done so, and it may have encouraged others to continue working who might have retired earlier. Their analysis of nine years of survey data indicates that the characteristics of retirement plans and their benefits have a substantial effect on whether phased retirement is attractive. Phased retirement is also differently attractive to more and less productive faculty, faculty at different types of institutions (for example, research versus comprehensive institutions), and faculty with health or other issues that affected their plans. The authors' survey data show high levels of satisfaction with the UNC's phased retirement policy and projects that increasing numbers will elect to phase in the foreseeable future. On balance, the system, the individual campuses, and the faculty who elect to phase all derive important benefits.

In Chapter Five, David Leslie draws on interview data from the Sloan study to assess the benefits and costs of phasing as perceived by those who elect this option and by deans and department chairs who supervise those who phase. The chapter also looks at individuals' motives to elect phased retirement, and at the social and psychological issues they confront as their positions and roles change. It concludes that the prime beneficiaries of phased retirement policies are individual faculty whose circumstances allow them to take full advantage of the opportunity. They can work less while still contributing to their institutions and professions, maintaining their connections and affiliations, but not suffering economically from downshifting. Institutions may find that phased retirement policies attract too many (or too few) faculty, perhaps disrupting some programs that lose more senior people than they had anticipated. In other cases, an insufficiently attractive plan may not encourage enough older faculty to consider the option. Some department chairs find that they assume more burdensome responsibilities to coordinate a less fully employed faculty, a potentially hidden cost of phased retirement.

In Chapter Six, David Leslie, Natasha Janson, and Valerie Martin Conley address the underlying policy challenge of balancing individual and institutional needs and interests. Among the most important issues facing policymakers in managing retirement programs are variability among faculty in the timing and manner of their retirements. Whereas national survey data provide a basis for estimating when and how current faculty expect to retire, the picture for future generations is not as clear. The authors explore implications of the data suggesting that earlier retirement will become more common, as will the demand for more flexible employment arrangements over entire careers. These trends will likely be reinforced by the preferences of women, who are now entering the academic workforce in far larger numbers than ever before. Financial constraints are also pressing institutions to minimize their long-term commitments to tenured faculty, while employing a more temporary and flexible workforce.

The chapter concludes that generational and gender changes in the faculty workforce, along with external pressures that have made it harder to compete for talent, will lead to policies that allow more flexible options for younger and older faculty alike. Because retirement is a profoundly individual process and because the choice to retire is now the individual's, and not under the institution's control, institutions need to learn how to support the retirement decision and process with options that lead to win-win outcomes for both individual and institution. Policy considerations that promote win-win outcomes are provided in the concluding section of this final chapter.

Reference

American Association of University Professors. *1940 Statement of Principles on Academic Freedom and Tenure with 1970 Interpretive Comments.* Washington, D.C.: American Association of University Professors, 2004. http://www.aaup.org/statements/Redbook/1940stat.htm.

DAVID W. LESLIE *is Chancellor Professor of Education at the College of William and Mary.*

VALERIE MARTIN CONLEY *is assistant professor of higher education and associate director of the Center for Higher Education at Ohio University.*

1

Faculty now have the task of using retirement options creatively, and institutions, of finding common purpose with faculty.

New Ways to Retire

David W. Leslie

Colleges and universities can no longer tell faculty when they must retire. Instead, faculty can now tell their institutions when they will retire. For years prior to 1994, the impending federal abolition of mandatory retirement caused colleges and universities to worry that faculty might choose never to retire. The specter of an infinitely aging and increasingly costly gerontocracy ruling the classrooms, labs, and committee structures of universities led to varied experiments with incentives and inducements to make retirement attractive to faculty members. In this issue of *New Directions for Higher Education,* we explore how one of those newer options, phased retirement, works.

The fears that faculty would take advantage of their privileges and stay on at their jobs indefinitely appear to have faded. On the whole, experience in the first decade following uncapping of mandatory retirement shows that faculty plan to retire in their mid-sixties and that only small numbers are likely to remain beyond age seventy. Faculty members vary in their careers, finances, and personal situations, though, and now must actively decide how to retire. Their employing institutions, once enforcers of a universal retirement age, increasingly recognize these factors and play the role of supporter, counselor, and adviser, offering options and negotiating terms and conditions under which faculty can choose the course they find best fits their circumstances.

The institution's role as a facilitator of retirement decisions is one that few have ever prepared to manage. Retirement is a once-in-a-lifetime transition for individuals. They may or may not have done more than the most rudimentary planning and may not have thought through the options

NEW DIRECTIONS FOR HIGHER EDUCATION, no. 132, Winter 2005 © Wiley Periodicals, Inc.
Published online in Wiley InterScience (www.interscience.wiley.com) • DOI: 10.1002/he.193

5

available to them. In addition, department chairs and deans, the frontline supervisors of faculty, are typically focused on building programs for the future, seeking funding, recruiting new faculty, and developing new courses of research and study. Although the orderly and inevitable departure of those who may have built the department in the past is a critical element in reshaping a department or college, chairs and deans have not typically been trained to deal with the concerns and issues facing prospective retirees.

In fact, very little in general is known about how to manage phased retirement issues in colleges and universities. The literature on faculty retirement is thin at best, so this volume will be one of the very few publications dealing with phased retirement. But as a large generation of faculty reaches their sixties, the need to understand who retires, why, when, and how is pressing.

Proportionally, the major concern of colleges and universities in the three or four decades after World War II was finding enough qualified faculty to fill positions in a rapidly expanding higher education system. Now a maturing industry, higher education is faced with a dramatically increasing number of faculty members in their late fifties and early sixties—those who were hired during the boom years of the 1960s and 1970s. And just as the tenured ranks have aged so quickly, so have institutions turned increasingly to temporary and part-time faculty as ways to put off making long-term financial commitments. Scarce state and federal funding and increasing tuition rates have limited institutions' ability to attract and hold newer Ph.D.s. Rapidly changing (and increasingly expensive) technology has also crimped institutions' ability to invest where new Ph.D.s feel it is professionally and scientifically important. So younger faculty appear to come and go in a far less permanent relationship to their institutions, while the tenured ranks age further without replacements. We have found that phased retirement helps both institutions and faculty in these circumstances.

For institutions, planning is made easier when they know who may be stepping down through a few years of partial employment and ultimately into retirement. Phased retirement can also provide an incentive to keep talented people from leaving too soon. (This is quite the opposite of what institutions may have thought they would need to do after the uncapping of mandatory retirement.) Also, faculty who phase into retirement accept reduced pay. The recovered funds can be redeployed to areas in which the institution needs to invest.

The individual faculty member benefits by easing through the transition to retirement and in several other obvious ways. Where institutions have provided for phased retirees to start receiving payouts from their retirement plans, those who do phase are often at least as well off financially as they were when working full time (see Chapter Four). They may continue their affiliation with their professional colleagues and continue to enjoy the life of the mind that has become for most a totally consuming way of life. Since many faculty lives are so fully engaged socially and psychologically in their institutions and professional activities, "cold turkey" retirement is both feared and difficult to manage. Phasing provides a transition both from this consuming involvement and to whatever may come next in a major shift in one's life course.

DAVID W. LESLIE *is Chancellor Professor of Education at the College of William and Mary.*

2

Late-career decisions are made by faculty who vary widely in career achievement, personal circumstances, and now, retirement patterns.

Demographics and Motives Affecting Faculty Retirement

Valerie Martin Conley

Population statistics and projections warn of an approaching crisis in the form of an aging professoriate (for example, Fogg, 2005; Lozier and Dooris, 1991; Rice and Finkelstein, 1993). In the light of these projections and the absence of mandatory retirement in academe, there has been widespread concern regarding whether sufficient incentives exist for faculty members to retire, while others worry that looming faculty retirements may impede higher education's ability to offer quality educational programs because qualified replacements may not exist. These alternative views are evident from the literature, which usually starts from one of two premises. While some researchers focus on increased demand in some disciplines and departments as institutions scramble to fill vacancies resulting from retirements (Hammond and Morgan, 1991; Holden and Hansen, 1989), others emphasize the impact that faculty members who postpone retirement indefinitely may have on an institution's ability to hire new faculty and restructure their program offerings (Daniels and Daniels, 1992; Lewis, 1996).

These points of view are important because although the decision about when to retire is an individual one, retirement is in part negotiated between the employer and the employee within the social context and legal boundaries that constrain it (Atchley, 1976). The extent to which administrators adhere to one viewpoint or another influences their willingness to negotiate with individuals approaching retirement.

In the aftermath of uncapping legislation, institutions (and systems) have experimented with an array of incentives, primarily to reduce uncertainty

NEW DIRECTIONS FOR HIGHER EDUCATION, no. 132, Winter 2005   © Wiley Periodicals, Inc.
Published online in Wiley InterScience (www.interscience.wiley.com) • DOI: 10.1002/he.194

about when individual faculty members will choose to retire. These incentive options take many forms, including early and phased retirement (Chronister and Kepple, 1987). Researchers have described many of the various incentive programs (Chronister and Kepple, 1987; Patton, 1983) and have identified some of the most important factors that influence when faculty members retire (Holden and Hansen, 2001). There is a lack of information on the effectiveness of the various incentive strategies, however. In other words, retirement incentives may or may not be needed, and they may or may not be successful in shaping faculty plans or behaviors.

From whatever perspective one views the uncapping of mandatory retirement, it has clearly shifted bargaining power to the individual, who is no longer required to retire at all. This shift in decision-making power was brought about by 1986 amendments to the U.S. Age Discrimination in Employment Act (ADEA). The shift sparked debate about the impact that eliminating mandatory retirement ages for tenured faculty (uncapping) would have on the academic labor market. Some researchers warned of inevitable shortages brought about by the unprecedented numbers of faculty who would be retiring in the near future. Others believed that progress toward diversifying the nation's faculty would be slowed as faculty delayed retirement indefinitely. Specifically, potential impacts of uncapping that were identified prior to the passage of the legislation included lower faculty turnover, an adverse affect on increasing diversity among the faculty ranks (in other words, a reduced ability to hire women and minorities), and increased costs associated with the continued employment of older faculty members (Hammond and Morgan, 1991).

In a more recent assessment of the impacts of uncapping, Clark and Hammond (2001) describe the environment after ADEA amendments as a "significantly altered academic labor market" (p. 1). They cite TIAA-CREF data indicating that some faculty are beginning to receive retirement income much earlier than their predecessors, while others are waiting much later to do so. They call for a national discussion regarding benefits and age discrimination laws, as well as the need for new evidence about the intended and unintended impact of these laws on institutions and individuals because faculty attitudes and perceptions regarding retirement and departure have not been comprehensively addressed since the legislation took effect on January 1, 1994.

In this chapter, I provide an overview of faculty attitudes toward retirement on a national scale some five years after the uncapping legislation took effect. This analysis relies on data gathered through the National Study of Postsecondary Faculty (NSOPF), which has been conducted approximately every five years beginning in 1988. In addition, estimates of retirement and turnover from the NSOPF:99 Institution Survey (the most recent data available at the time of this writing) provide a context for understanding retirement issues facing higher education today. Data from the NSOPF:99 Faculty

Survey describe the attitudes of faculty in general and help to answer questions including:

- How old are faculty members on average?
- How many faculty members retired on average between the fall of 1997 and the fall of 1998?
- What percentage of older faculty members are very likely to retire in the next three years?
- Were there differences in the retirement plans of faculty by program area?
- Did some types of institutions experience more retirements on average than others?
- How are men and women alike or different in their retirement plans?
- Are particular disciplines more or less affected by short-term retirement plans?
- Do faculty members in research institutions have different attitudes about the age they were most likely to retire than faculty in other types of institutions?

This last question is crucial given the arguments that were made in opposition to uncapping, which warned that research institutions in particular would be faced with a substantial number of aging tenured faculty members and would be forced to look for alternatives to traditional tenure-track positions to fulfill their missions (Hammond and Morgan, 1991).

The chapter begins with estimates of retirements between fall 1997 and fall 1998 using data taken from the NSOPF:99 Institution Survey. Next, trends in the age distribution of full-time instructional faculty and staff are given using data from the 1988, 1993, and 1999 NSOPF, and detailed information is provided on selected demographic and employment characteristics of faculty in fall 1998. Next, faculty retirement plans are described generally, including the likelihood of retiring in the next three years, the number of years faculty expect to continue working before retiring, and the age they expect to retire from all paid employment. In this section, some of the potential motives for retiring are also examined. Finally, receptivity to early or phased retirement is explored. Because employment status (whether the individual is employed full or part time by the institution) is tied to the types of benefits (including retirement) received from institutions, the analyses in this chapter include only instructional faculty and staff members who are employed full time by their institutions. In addition, because the context of the work environment and informal norms about work influence retirement decisions (Atchley, 1976; Ekerdt, DeViney, and Kosloski, 1996; Szinovacz and DeViney, 2000), most of the analyses in this chapter focus on faculty in four-year institutions. Some data for full-time faculty in two-year institutions are selectively provided.

Estimates of Retirements

Data from the NSOPF:99 institution survey indicate that about fourteen thousand (2.5 percent on average) full-time faculty and instructional staff retired between fall 1997 and fall 1998 (U.S. Department of Education, 1999). Twenty-nine percent of all those who left institutions that year did so to retire (Berger, Kirshstein, and Rowe, 2001). Some institutions experienced more retirements than others, however. The number of retirees across four-year institutions with any retirements ranged from a minimum of 1 to a maximum of 389 (U.S. Department of Education, 1999). Public two-year institutions had the highest proportion of retirements (50 percent) compared to other institutional types, including, for example, public research institutions (21 percent), private research institutions (12 percent), and private liberal arts institutions (32 percent) (Berger, Kirshstein, and Rowe, 2001). Most institutions (70 percent of four-year and 64 percent of two-year institutions, respectively) had at least one faculty member retire between the 1997 and 1998 fall terms. During the preceding five years (fall 1993 to fall 1998), 32 percent of institutions with tenure systems offered early or phased retirement to at least one tenured full-time faculty or instructional staff member. In institutions with a tenure system offering early retirement, an average of 6.5 percent took early retirement during the past five years (U.S. Department of Education, 1999).

Demographic and Employment Characteristics

There were about 1.07 million faculty and instructional staff employed by public and private nonprofit two-year-and-above Title IV degree-granting postsecondary institutions in fall 1998. Most (about 976,000) reported having some instructional responsibilities for credit, including teaching classes for credit or advising students about academic activities for credit. Among these individuals (referred to as instructional faculty and staff), 57 percent were employed full time, and 43 percent were employed part time (Zimbler, 2001). Approximately 450,000 instructional faculty and staff were employed full time in four-year institutions, and roughly 110,000 were employed full time in two-year institutions.

Full-time instructional faculty and staff were forty-nine years old on average in the fall of 1998 (Table 2.1). Close to one-third (31 percent) of full-time faculty members were fifty-five years old or older. Five percent were sixty-five to seventy years old. One percent of full-time faculty members were seventy-one or older. Although a higher percentage of full-time instructional faculty and staff in four-year institutions were sixty-five to seventy years old (5 percent) than in two-year institutions (3 percent), there was little substantive difference in the average age by type of institution, suggesting similar age distributions overall.

Table 2.1. Average Age and Age Distribution of Full-Time Instructional Faculty and Staff, by Tenure Status, Academic Rank, Gender, and Race/Ethnicity: Fall 1998

Tenure Status, Academic Rank, Gender, and Race/Ethnicity	Average Age	Age Distribution					
		Under 35	35 to 44	45 to 54	55 to 64	65 to 70	71 or Older
All full-time instructional faculty and staff in degree-granting institutions[1]	49.2	7.3	25.3	36.0	25.9	4.5	1.0
Tenure status							
Tenured	53.1	0.9	15.4	39.3	36.1	6.8	1.5
Not tenured/no tenure system	44.8	14.7	36.6	32.2	14.3	1.8	0.5
Academic rank							
Full professor	55.5	0.6	6.7	36.3	44.7	9.5	2.2
Associate professor	49.7	1.1	27.6	44.6	22.4	3.8	0.5
Assistant professor	42.9	16.0	45.7	27.1	9.9	1.1	0.3
All other ranks/not applicable	46.3	14.2	28.1	35.3	20.1	1.8	0.7
Gender							
Male	50.2	6.1	23.8	33.5	29.8	5.7	1.2
Female	47.4	9.5	28.0	40.3	19.1	2.4	0.8
Race/ethnicity							
American Indian/Alaska Native	46.9	6.9	36.1	39.6	14.8	2.0	0.7
Asian/Pacific Islander	46.1	9.3	38.4	31.4	15.5	4.3	1.1
Black, non-Hispanic	48.6	6.8	25.5	40.9	22.6	3.3	0.9
Hispanic	45.6	11.7	35.7	35.3	13.2	3.0	1.1
White, non-Hispanic	49.6	7.1	23.9	36.0	27.4	4.6	1.0

[1]All public and private, not-for-profit Title IV participating, degree-granting institutions in the fifty states and the District of Columbia.

Note: This table includes only faculty and staff with instructional responsibilities for credit (such as teaching one or more classes for credit, or advising or supervising students' academic activities). Percentages may not total to 100 because of rounding.

Source: U.S. Department of Education, National Center for Education Statistics, 1999 National Study of Postsecondary Faculty (NSOPF:99).

There is ample evidence to support a general graying of the professoriate. The average age of faculty has increased steadily since the fall of 1987. Full-time instructional faculty and staff were forty-seven years old on average in the fall of 1987, forty-eight years old on average in the fall of 1992, and forty-nine years old on average in the fall of 1998 (U.S. Department of Education, n.d.). Contributing to an increase in the average age, there has been an increase in the percentage of faculty who were fifty-five to fifty-nine years old since the fall of 1987 and a decrease in the percentage of faculty under forty-four years old during the time period. There was also an increase in the percentage of faculty members who were seventy or older between the fall of 1987 (0.5 percent) and the fall of 1998 (1 percent).

Taken together, these data lend support to a concern put forth by the higher education community during the congressional hearings on ending mandatory retirement ages as part of the ADEA amendments: that the changes in legislation coupled with the existence of tenure could severely limit institutions' ability to hire new faculty (Hammond and Morgan, 1991).

Data do not entirely support another concern voiced during the hearings, however. Some thought there would be an adverse effect on increasing diversity among the faculty ranks (a reduced ability to hire women and minorities). What do the data tell us? Female faculty members were younger on average than their male colleagues in the fall of 1998 (Table 2.1). Yet the average age has increased for both men and women. Men were forty-eight years old on average in the fall of 1987, forty-nine years old on average in the fall of 1992, and fifty years old on average in the fall of 1998. The increase for women was from forty-five years old on average in the fall of 1987, to forty-six years old on average in the fall of 1993, to forty-seven years old on average in the fall of 1998 (U.S. Department of Education, n.d.).

Just as men were older than women on average in the fall of 1998, so were white, non-Hispanic faculty members older on average than faculty of other ethnicities, except for blacks (where no statistically significant difference was observed). The average age of blacks increased from forty-six years old in the fall of 1987 to forty-seven years old in the fall of 1992 to forty-nine years old in the fall of 1998 (U.S. Department of Education, n.d.).

If younger faculty were being hired from underrepresented groups, we might expect the average age for these groups to decrease or at least hold steady. However, faculty may be older when they are hired into their positions. It is not possible to determine from the available data whether this is the case.

But looking at aggregate data on age by gender and race/ethnicity tells only part of the story. The academic labor market is characterized by segmentation among institution types and academic disciplines (Clark, 1997). The average age of faculty varies from forty-eight years old on average in private, nonprofit doctoral-granting institutions to fifty-one years old on average in public comprehensive institutions. The average age of faculty in public two-year institutions was forty-nine (Table 2.2). Recent research on retirement issues in public two-year institutions points out that the average age has increased for both full- and part-time faculty in these institutions, but the rate of increase has been greater for those employed part time (Conley, forthcoming). Similar variations are evident by academic field. The age of faculty varies from forty-eight years old on average in health sciences to fifty-one years old on average in education (Table 2.2).

NEW DIRECTIONS FOR HIGHER EDUCATION • DOI 10.1002/he

Table 2.2. Average Age and Age Distribution of Full-Time Instructional Faculty and Staff, by Institution Type and Program Area: Fall 1998

Institution Type and Program Area	Average Age	Under 35	35 to 44	45 to 54	55 to 64	65 to 70	71 or Older
		Age Distribution					
All full-time instructional faculty and staff in degree-granting institutions[1]	49.2	7.3	25.3	36.0	25.9	4.5	1.0
Public research	48.8	7.6	27.4	34.6	24.2	5.3	0.8
Private not-for-profit research	48.8	8.1	28.3	32.3	24.0	5.8	1.7
Public doctoral[2]	49.0	7.0	28.4	33.9	24.2	5.6	0.8
Private not-for-profit doctoral[2]	47.8	8.8	29.6	36.4	21.0	3.2	1.0
Public comprehensive	50.6	6.2	21.7	34.0	31.3	5.7	1.1
Private not-for-profit comprehensive	49.5	8.0	21.9	37.4	28.6	3.5	0.6
Private not-for-profit liberal arts	48.3	8.7	29.6	33.0	24.1	3.7	1.0
Public 2-year	49.3	6.5	21.9	41.2	27.1	2.3	0.9
Other[3]	49.3	7.2	22.9	40.3	23.6	4.0	2.0
Public institutions	49.3	7.0	24.7	36.3	26.6	4.5	0.9
Public 4-year doctoral institutions	48.9	7.5	27.7	34.4	24.2	5.4	0.8
Public 4-year nondoctoral institutions	50.3	6.6	21.6	34.8	30.9	5.1	1.0
Public 2-year institutions	49.3	6.5	21.9	41.2	27.1	2.3	0.9
Private not-for-profit institutions	48.8	8.1	26.9	35.2	24.2	4.3	1.3
Private 4-year doctoral institutions	48.4	8.3	28.7	33.7	22.9	4.9	1.5
Private 4-year nondoctoral institutions	49.0	7.6	26.4	36.3	24.8	3.7	1.3
Private 2-year institutions	49.6	15.8	12.8	32.1	28.9	9.0	1.4
All program areas in 4-year institutions[4]	49.1	7.4	26.3	34.8	25.6	4.9	1.0
Agriculture/home economics	50.3	9.0	16.8	36.3	32.6	4.8	0.5
Business	48.8	5.6	28.0	38.6	24.1	3.1	0.6
Education	50.7	5.7	16.8	40.3	31.5	5.2	0.5
Engineering	48.3	10.5	29.0	29.4	24.7	5.4	1.1
Fine arts	49.1	5.1	26.7	40.3	23.8	3.6	0.6
Health sciences	47.6	6.0	33.2	37.3	19.4	3.3	0.8
Humanities	50.1	8.6	22.0	31.0	30.1	7.1	1.2
Natural sciences	49.3	7.1	28.8	32.2	24.3	6.2	1.5
Social sciences	49.1	8.5	25.8	32.0	29.2	3.1	1.4
All other fields	49.2	9.1	22.7	36.6	25.1	5.5	1.0

[1]All public and private, not-for-profit Title IV participating, degree-granting institutions in the fifty states and the District of Columbia.

[2]Includes institutions classified by the Carnegie Foundation as specialized medical schools and medical centers.

[3]Public liberal arts, private 2-year, and other specialized institutions except medical schools and medical centers.

[4]Includes public liberal arts, and other specialized institutions not separately identified, but included within "other."

Note: This table includes only faculty and staff with instructional responsibilities for credit (such as teaching one or more classes for credit, or advising or supervising students' academic activities). Percentages may not total to 100 because of rounding.

Source: U.S. Department of Education, National Center for Education Statistics, 1999 National Study of Postsecondary Faculty (NSOPF:99).

Retirement Plans and Motives for Retiring

Although age is one of the strongest predictors of when an individual will decide to retire (Palmore, 1971), faculty members are influenced by a complex set of factors when making this decision. Some of these are financial (see, for example, Gustman and Steinmeir, 1991, and Lewis, 1996) while others are nonfinancial (see, for example, Monahan and Greene, 1987; Lozier and Dooris, 1991; Costa, 1998; Szinovacz and DeViney, 2000; and Holden and Hansen, 2001).

Daniels and Daniels (1992) distinguished between factors that acted to push faculty members toward retirement and those that pulled or kept them from making the decision to retire. Generally push factors make continued employment unrewarding or unpleasant (push the individual toward retirement) and pull factors make continued employment a more attractive option than retirement (pull the individual away from retirement).

Money as a factor in the retirement decision matters to nearly everyone, but researchers have reached different conclusions regarding the relative importance of finances in the decision about when to retire (Costa, 1998; Gray, 1989; Lewis, 1996; Lozier and Dooris, 1991; Monahan and Greene, 1987). For example, Lozier and Dooris (1991) found overall financial status and eligibility for full retirement benefits were the most important predictors of retirement among faculty. However, Costa (1998) provided evidence suggesting that monetary factors being equal, nonmonetary factors help to explain why some people retire sooner than others. Gray (1989) found that an adequate retirement income is a necessary condition but not a sufficient reason for retirement: "Other factors are more likely to trigger the actual decision as to when to retire" (p. 7). NSOPF:99 did not collect information that could be used to assess financial status or eligibility for full retirement benefits. This is a limitation of the study.

This limitation, however, does not negate the importance of the information that is contained in the data set, though. Keefe (2001) urges academic administrators to place an equal emphasis on the intangible aspects of retirement when designing retirement incentives. There is evidence to suggest that a poor fit between faculty members and their institutions, feelings of alienation from the academic department or from the institution, a lack of collegiality, and dissatisfaction may factor importantly in the retirement decision (Dey, Vander Putten, Han, and Coles, 1997; Dorfman, 2002; Durbin, Gross, and Borgatta, 1984; Holden and Hansen, 1989; Hanisch and Hulin, 1990; Monahan and Greene, 1987). Individual faculty members identified an increase in bureaucratization, a lack of appreciation for the human element of the job, and less autonomy as reasons for retiring when they did (Dorfman, 2002).

Furthermore, professional roles and activities have been associated with the decision to retire or continue working among older faculty members. A large majority of those who continue to work do so because of intrinsic rewards (Dorfman, 2002; Hammond and Morgan, 1991; Rees and Smith, 1991; Smith, 1991).

NSOPF:99 includes several items related to the intangible aspects of retirement. The focus of this section is on these aspects, specifically retirement plans and motives for retiring. Analyses will be limited to faculty members fifty-five years old or older because older faculty members are more certain about when they will retire than younger faculty members (Chronister, Baldwin, and Conley, 1997). As noted earlier, 31 percent of faculty members were fifty-five or older in the fall of 1998 (Table 2.1).

The Next Three Years. One-quarter (25 percent) of faculty members fifty-five or older reported that they were very likely to retire in the next three years. An additional one-quarter (24 percent) were somewhat likely to retire. Nineteen percent of all full-time instructional faculty and staff had at least some plans to retire (Table 2.3).

Reflecting the age distribution of faculty by gender and ethnicity, male faculty members (10 percent) were more likely than female faculty members (7 percent) to report they were very likely to retire in the next three years, and a higher proportion of white, non-Hispanic faculty members were very likely to retire in the next three years than other racial/ethnic groups with the exception of black, non-Hispanic faculty. The more satisfied that faculty members age fifty-five and older reported being with workload, job security, salary, and time available for keeping current in the field, the more likely they were to report that they were very likely to retire in the next three years (Table 2.3).

Generally as income increased, the percentage of faculty indicating they were very likely to retire in the next three years decreased. For example, 28 percent of faculty members with total income from the institution between $40,000 and $69,999 reported they were very likely to retire in the next three years, while 13 percent of faculty members with total income from the institution between $115,000 and $129,999 and 10 percent of faculty members with total income from the institution of $130,000 or more reported intentions to do so (Table 2.4). Similarly, faculty members with higher salaries were generally more likely to report not having retirement plans in the next three years. However, faculty members who earned less and faculty who earned more did not fit the mold, suggesting nonfinancial factors may be playing a significant role in their decision about when to retire. Because higher income is generally associated with higher productivity, a combination of structural-functional analysis using disengagement theory and symbolic-interaction analysis drawing on activity theory may shed light on these relationships. Further research is needed to understand the complex relationship between satisfaction and income and their influence on retirement decision making in the context of the contemporary environment.

Age of Expected Retirement. Another way of assessing plans for retirement is to ask faculty members at what age they expect to retire. Estimated retirement ages may be a good approximation for actual retirement ages.

Table 2.3. Percentage Distribution of Full-Time Instructional Faculty and Staff Age 55 and Older, by Likelihood of Retiring in the Next Three Years, and by Satisfaction with Various Work Conditions: Fall 1998

Satisfaction with Various Work Conditions	Retire from the Labor Force in the Next Three Years		
	Not at All Likely	Somewhat Likely	Very Likely
All full-time instructional faculty and staff in degree-granting institutions*	81.2	10.1	8.7
Age 55 and older	51.1	24.4	24.6
Workload			
Very dissatisfied	53.8	27.5	18.7
Somewhat dissatisfied	52.6	27.7	19.7
Somewhat satisfied	51.4	23.0	25.7
Very satisfied	49.4	23.4	27.3
Job security			
Very dissatisfied	56.7	24.7	18.7
Somewhat dissatisfied	55.6	28.9	15.5
Somewhat satisfied	55.5	24.9	19.6
Very satisfied	48.8	23.7	27.5
Salary			
Very dissatisfied	53.4	26.8	19.8
Somewhat dissatisfied	55.2	22.7	22.2
Somewhat satisfied	49.0	25.2	25.9
Very satisfied	48.9	23.0	28.1
Time available for keeping current in my field			
Very dissatisfied	57.4	21.3	21.3
Somewhat dissatisfied	52.1	27.8	20.1
Somewhat satisfied	49.2	24.1	26.6
Very satisfied	49.4	21.6	29.0

*All public and private, not-for-profit Title IV participating, degree-granting institutions in the fifty states and the District of Columbia.

Note: This table includes only faculty and staff with instructional responsibilities for credit (such as teaching one or more classes for credit, or advising or supervising students' academic activities). Percentages may not total to 100 because of rounding.

Source: U.S. Department of Education, National Center for Education Statistics, 1999 National Study of Postsecondary Faculty (NSOPF:99).

Berry, Hammons, and Denny (2001) found, for example, that "faculty members' estimated retirement ages differed only slightly from C[hief] A[cademic] O[fficer]s' observations of recent retirement patterns" (p. 130). Tables 2.5 and 2.6 provide the percentage distribution of faculty members by the number of years they expected to work before they retire and the age at which they expected to retire, respectively.

NEW DIRECTIONS FOR HIGHER EDUCATION • DOI 10.1002/he

Table 2.4. Percentage Distribution of Full-Time Instructional Faculty and Staff Age 55 and Older, by Likelihood of Retiring in the Next Three Years, and by Income, Number of Dependents, and Geographic Region: Fall 1998

Income, Number of Dependents, and Geographic Region	Retire from the Labor Force in the Next Three Years		
	Not at All Likely	Somewhat Likely	Very Likely
All full-time instructional faculty and staff in degree-granting institutions[1]	81.2	10.1	8.7
Age 55 and older	51.1	24.4	24.6
Income[2]			
Less than $40,000	52.3	23.2	24.6
$40,000–$69,999	49.0	23.3	27.8
$70,000–$99,999	49.9	26.7	23.4
$100,000–$114,999	53.9	24.6	21.5
$115,000–$129,999	70.7	16.3	13.0
$130,000 or more	59.7	30.7	9.6
Number of dependents			
None	47.4	26.2	26.3
1 to 3	53.1	22.9	24.0
4 or more	69.1	20.9	10.0
Geographic region			
New England	62.5	19.8	17.7
Mideast	51.4	23.3	25.4
Great lakes	49.3	26.1	24.6
Plains	48.7	22.6	28.6
Southeast	52.0	25.3	22.8
Southwest	48.5	27.7	23.8
Rocky Mountain	49.5	25.4	25.1
Far West	50.1	22.8	27.1

[1]All public and private, not-for-profit Title IV participating, degree-granting institutions in the fifty states and the District of Columbia.

[2]Total income from the institution.

Note: This table includes only faculty and staff with instructional responsibilities for credit (such as teaching one or more classes for credit, or advising or supervising students' academic activities). Percentages may not total to 100 because of rounding.

Source: U.S. Department of Education, National Center for Education Statistics, 1999 National Study of Postsecondary Faculty (NSOPF:99).

In the fall of 1998, the overwhelming majority of faculty age fifty-five or older (94 percent) expected to work no more than fifteen years until retirement. More than a third, 36 percent, of faculty age fifty-five or older expected to work only one to five years until retirement (Table 2.5). Thirty-eight percent expected to work between six and ten more years until retirement.

Table 2.5. Percentage Distribution of Full-Time Instructional Faculty and Staff, by Number of Years Until Retirement, and by Age, Tenure Status, Academic Rank, Gender, and Race/Ethnicity: Fall 1998

Tenure Status, Academic Rank, Gender, and Race/Ethnicity	Years Until Retirement					
	1 to 5	6 to 10	11 to 15	16 to 20	21 to 25	Over 25
All full-time instructional faculty and staff in degree-granting institutions*	11.9	16.7	18.2	18.2	14.9	20.1
Age						
Under 55	1.6	7.6	18.0	23.9	20.8	28.2
55 and older	36.4	38.4	18.8	4.4	1.0	0.9
Tenure status						
Tenured	16.9	22.3	22.0	18.1	11.9	8.9
Not tenured/no tenure system	6.3	10.5	14.1	18.3	18.4	32.5
Academic rank						
Full professor	20.8	25.9	23.5	15.5	8.9	5.5
Associate professor	10.4	16.0	19.7	22.1	17.5	14.4
Assistant professor	4.6	7.6	10.6	17.8	19.6	39.9
All other ranks/not applicable	9.1	14.5	17.4	18.0	15.6	25.4
Gender						
Male	14.0	17.4	18.0	17.7	14.6	18.4
Female	8.2	15.4	18.7	19.0	15.6	23.2
Race/ethnicity						
American Indian/Alaska Native	6.7	14.5	20.4	22.3	14.9	21.2
Asian/Pacific Islander	9.6	9.2	12.0	23.2	21.7	24.2
Black, non-Hispanic	11.0	15.0	21.9	19.8	13.0	19.4
Hispanic	5.9	10.1	16.6	19.5	16.7	31.4
White, non-Hispanic	12.3	17.6	18.5	17.7	14.5	19.4

*All public and private, not-for-profit Title IV participating, degree-granting institutions in the fifty states and the District of Columbia.

Note: This table includes only faculty and staff with instructional responsibilities for credit (such as teaching one or more classes for credit, or advising or supervising students' academic activities). Percentages may not total to 100 because of rounding.

Source: U.S. Department of Education, National Center for Education Statistics, 1999 National Study of Postsecondary Faculty (NSOPF:99).

Nineteen percent of faculty age fifty-five or older expected to work between eleven and fifteen more years before retirement (Table 2.5).

The average age at which full-time instructional faculty and staff expected to retire from all paid employment was sixty-six (Table 2.6). But younger faculty members expected to retire at an earlier age on average than their older colleagues. The average age at which full-time tenured faculty members under age thirty-five expected to retire from all paid employment was sixty-four years old (Table 2.6). However, there is also less certainty

Table 2.6. Age at Which Full-Time Instructional Faculty and Staff Expect to Retire from All Paid Employment, by Current Age, Tenure Status, and Institution Type: Fall 1998

Age, Tenure Status, and Institution Type	Average Age Expecting to Retire	Percentage Expecting to Retire at Age			
		55 to 59	60 to 64	65 to 70	71 or Older
All full-time instructional faculty and staff in degree-granting institutions*	65.9	9.7	21.0	56.7	12.6
Age					
Under 35	64.2	19.3	21.7	48.6	10.4
35 to 44	64.7	15.1	22.3	53.1	9.5
45 to 54	65.6	10.2	21.8	57.4	10.6
55 to 64	66.8	3.0	23.0	61.9	12.1
65 to 70	70.6			67.4	32.6
71 or older	76.7				100.0
Tenure status					
Tenured	65.4	7.1	20.7	58.2	14.0
Not tenured/no tenure system	66.4	12.6	21.4	55.1	11.0
Public institutions	65.6	10.5	22.0	55.9	11.6
Public 4-year doctoral institutions	66.1	9.8	18.0	58.9	13.2
Public 4-year nondoctoral institutions	65.7	9.9	22.2	56.4	11.5
Public 2-year institutions	64.6	12.4	29.3	49.7	8.6
Private not-for-profit institutions	66.6	7.7	18.8	58.7	14.9
Private 4-year doctoral institutions	67.3	6.7	16.6	59.3	17.3
Private 4-year nondoctoral institutions	66.3	8.3	19.7	58.6	13.5
Private 2-year institutions	66.3	6.7	26.4	53.1	13.8

*All public and private, not-for-profit Title IV participating, degree-granting institutions in the fifty states and the District of Columbia.

Note: This table includes only faculty and staff with instructional responsibilities for credit (such as teaching one or more classes for credit, or advising or supervising students' academic activities). Percentages may not total to 100 because of rounding.

Source: U.S. Department of Education, National Center for Education Statistics, 1999 National Study of Postsecondary Faculty (NSOPF:99).

among younger faculty members about the age at which they will retire (Chronister, Baldwin, and Conley, 1997).

More faculty members report planning to retire between ages sixty-five and seventy than in any other age group. But more faculty members at private, nonprofit institutions (15 percent) expected to retire at age seventy-one or older than faculty members in public institutions (12 percent) (Table 2.6). Conversely, a higher percentage of faculty members in public institutions than private institutions expected to retire between the ages of fifty-five and sixty-four. More faculty at public two-year institutions plan to retire earlier and fewer plan to retire later than faculty at other types of institutions, suggesting that the context for retirement decision-making is different in two-year and four-year institutions.

Faculty members in private nonprofit institutions expected to retire one year later on average than faculty at public institutions. The average age faculty in private institutions expected to retire at was sixty-seven, while the average age faculty in public institutions expected to retire at was sixty-six (Table 2.6). Faculty members in private nonprofit institutions also indicated they expected to work longer before retiring than faculty in public institutions did.

These data illustrate the importance of the institutional context in understanding issues related to faculty retirement. While large numbers of faculty are not expected to retire at any given point in time, individual institutions may experience higher or lower rates of retirement than others. Public and nonresearch-oriented institutions are more likely to experience higher rates of retirement (and earlier retirements among younger faculty) than private and research-oriented institutions.

Receptivity to Early and Phased Retirement Options. Although institutions may no longer impose mandatory retirement ages for tenured faculty members, institutions may offer voluntary retirement incentive programs. The extent to which institutions choose to offer such programs affects individuals' retirement decisions (Chronister and Kepple, 1987).

Nearly half of all colleges and universities (40 percent in 1993 and 47 percent in 1998) offered early or phased retirement options to tenured faculty during the five years preceding the two most recent NSOPF surveys. Institutions with higher proportions of tenured faculty were more likely to offer early or phased retirement options (U.S. Department of Education, 1993, 1999). The range of options available may affect individual faculty members' choices, possibly in systematic ways.

Retirement Options

The remainder of the chapter focuses on various retirement options, including early and phased retirement.

Early Retirement. A higher percentage of those who are closest to but have not yet reached the traditional retirement age of sixty-five said they were willing to take early retirement than those who were sixty-five or older. More than half of those age fifty-five to sixty-four (54 percent) said they were willing to take early retirement compared with 41 percent and 31 percent in the older age groups (ages sixty-five to seventy and seventy-one and older, respectively) (Table 2.7). Those in the older age groups may feel they have passed an age where their retirement would be considered early. Yet institutions may also couch retirement incentive programs or buyouts in terms of early retirement. The vagueness of the question wording makes it difficult to discern how respondents may have interpreted it. Nonetheless, a higher percentage of women (50 percent) than men (45 percent) indicated a willingness to take

Table 2.7. Percentage Distribution of Full-Time Instructional Faculty and Staff, by Willingness to Take an Early Retirement Option from Their Institution If Offered, and by Age, Tenure Status, Academic Rank, Gender, and Race/Ethnicity: Fall 1998

Age, Tenure Status, Academic Rank, Gender, and Race/Ethnicity	Percentage Willing to Take Early Retirement	
	Yes	No
All full-time instructional faculty and staff in degree-granting institutions*	46.9	53.1
Age		
Under 35	40.5	59.5
35 to 44	43.3	56.7
45 to 54	46.2	53.8
55 to 64	54.2	45.8
65 to 70	40.9	59.1
71 or older	30.7	69.3
Under 55	44.6	55.4
55 or older	51.3	48.7
Tenure status		
Tenured	49.2	50.8
Not tenured/no tenure system	44.1	55.9
Academic Rank		
Full professor	48.5	51.5
Associate professor	44.5	55.5
Assistant professor	42.7	57.3
All other ranks/not applicable	50.9	49.1
Gender		
Male	45.1	54.9
Female	50.4	49.6
Race/ethnicity		
American Indian/Alaska Native	48.0	52.0
Asian/Pacific Islander	43.2	56.8
Black, non-Hispanic	46.9	53.2
Hispanic	43.4	56.6
White, non-Hispanic	47.3	52.7

*All public and private, not-for-profit Title IV participating, degree-granting institutions in the fifty states and the District of Columbia.

Note: This table includes only faculty and staff with instructional responsibilities for credit (such as teaching one or more classes for credit, or advising or supervising students' academic activities). Percentages may not total to 100 because of rounding.

Source: U.S. Department of Education, National Center for Education Statistics, 1999 National Study of Postsecondary Faculty (NSOPF:99).

an early retirement option. About half of tenured faculty (49 percent) and slightly less than half (48 percent) of full professors would be willing to take such an option (Table 2.7).

Again, institutional context is important. Thirty-eight percent of faculty members in public two-year institutions were willing to take an early retirement option compared with 28 percent of faculty in public research and 23 percent of faculty in private research institutions (Table 2.8). Across all types of institutions, about one-third of faculty members were unsure if they would take early retirement. Although respondents were not given the option "it depends," it may be that the circumstances related to what early retirement means within the particular institutional setting may weigh in the decision.

However, these data suggest many senior faculty members may be willing to take an early retirement incentive option from their institution if one were offered to them. The data also highlight the ambiguity associated with human resource planning that academic administrators are facing now that mandatory retirement has been eliminated.

Early retirement incentive options have become more prevalent since the ADEA amendments took effect (Chronister and Kepple, 1987). However, early retirement options provide just one example of how institutions have encouraged faculty members to retire.

Phased Retirement. Many institutions offer more flexible work arrangements and have recognized the transitional nature of retirement. Some of these institutions have implemented phased retirement policies. The most notable such program is the California State University system's Faculty Early Retirement Program.

NSOPF data show that 54 percent of full-time faculty members age fifty-five or older would consider drawing on retirement income while continuing to work part time at their institution (Table 2.9). Fifty-eight percent of faculty seventy-one or older, 57 percent of faculty sixty-five to seventy, and 53 percent of faculty fifty-five to sixty-four would do so (Table 2.9). Both male and female faculty were more likely to be interested in drawing on retirement income and continuing to work part time than not. A higher percentage of faculty members in public two-year institutions (53 percent) than in public four-year doctoral institutions (45 percent) would elect to draw on retirement income while continuing to work part time at their institutions (U.S. Department of Education, n.d.).

In addition to phased retirement, faculty members are also engaged in bridge employment or postcareer labor force participation (Ruhm, 1990). There is some evidence to suggest that faculty may be opting to participate in phased retirement plans that allow them to convert to part-time status and begin to draw retirement income. Some faculty may be retiring from one institution to go to work for another. Nine percent of faculty had previously retired from another position (Table 2.10). The majority of these faculty members (74 percent) were employed part time (U.S. Department of Education, n.d.).

NEW DIRECTIONS FOR HIGHER EDUCATION • DOI 10.1002/he

Table 2.8. Percentage Distribution of Full-Time Instructional Faculty and Staff, by Willingness to Accept an Early Retirement Option from Their Institution If Offered, and by Institution Type and Program Area: Fall 1998

Institution Type and Program Area	Percentage Willing to Take Early Retirement		
	Yes	No	Don't Know
All full-time instructional faculty and staff in degree-granting institutions[1]	31.1	35.2	33.8
Public not-for-profit research	28.5	36.8	34.8
Private research	23.4	41.3	35.3
Public doctoral[2]	32.2	34.7	33.1
Private not-for-profit doctoral[2]	26.4	41.0	32.6
Public comprehensive	36.1	32.0	31.9
Private not-for-profit comprehensive	24.9	37.6	37.6
Private not-for-profit liberal arts	28.2	35.8	36.0
Public 2-year	38.2	30.0	31.8
Other[3]	28.4	38.5	33.1
All program areas in 4-year institutions[4]	29.4	36.3	34.3
Agriculture/home economics	31.6	22.9	45.5
Business	31.3	39.5	29.2
Education	31.3	36.7	32.0
Engineering	26.1	39.1	34.7
Fine arts	32.0	34.7	33.4
Health sciences	28.8	34.4	36.8
Humanities	28.7	36.6	34.7
Natural sciences	27.7	36.1	36.2
Social sciences	27.4	37.6	35.0
All other fields	32.4	39.1	28.5

[1]All public and private, not-for-profit Title IV participating, degree-granting institutions in the fifty states and the District of Columbia.

[2]Includes institutions classified by the Carnegie Foundation as specialized medical schools and medical centers.

[3]Public liberal arts, private 2-year, and other specialized institutions except medical schools and medical centers.

[4]Includes public liberal arts, and specialized institutions not separately identified, but included within "other."

Note: This table includes all full-time faculty (regardless of whether they had instructional responsibilities) and all other instructional staff. Percentages may not total to 100 because of rounding.

Source: U.S. Department of Education, National Center for Education Statistics, 1999 National Study of Postsecondary Faculty (NSOPF:99).

Table 2.9. Percentage Distribution of Full-Time Instructional Faculty and Staff, by Interest in Electing to Draw on Retirement Income and Continue Working at Their Institution on a Part-Time Basis, and by Age, Tenure Status, Academic Rank, Gender, and Race/Ethnicity: Fall 1998

Age, Tenure Status, Academic Rank, Gender, and Race/Ethnicity	Percentage Interested in Drawing on Retirement Income		
	Yes	No	Don't Know
All full-time instructional faculty and staff in degree-granting institutions*	47.3	29.4	23.3
Age			
Under 35	35.1	31.0	33.9
35 to 44	41.2	33.6	25.2
45 to 54	48.6	28.4	23.0
55 to 64	53.1	27.2	19.7
65 to 70	56.6	24.6	18.7
71 or older	57.8	26.1	16.1
Under 55	44.4	30.6	25.0
55 or older	53.7	26.8	19.5
Tenure status			
Tenured	49.1	29.6	21.3
Not tenured/no tenure system	45.3	29.2	25.5
Academic Rank			
Full professor	50.9	28.6	20.4
Associate professor	45.6	30.6	23.9
Assistant professor	41.9	31.5	26.6
All other ranks/not applicable	49.6	27.3	23.1
Gender			
Male	48.1	30.1	21.8
Female	45.9	28.3	25.8
Race/ethnicity			
American Indian/Alaska Native	42.4	28.6	29.0
Asian/Pacific Islander	46.5	27.8	25.8
Black, non-Hispanic	48.3	34.9	16.8
Hispanic	49.0	29.4	21.6
White, non-Hispanic	47.3	29.2	23.5

*All public and private, not-for-profit Title IV participating, degree-granting institutions in the fifty states and the District of Columbia.

Note: This table includes only faculty and staff with instructional responsibilities for credit (such as teaching one or more classes for credit, or advising or supervising students' academic activities). Percentages may not total to 100 because of rounding.

Source: U.S. Department of Education, National Center for Education Statistics, 1999 National Study of Postsecondary Faculty (NSOPF:99).

Table 2.10. Percentage Distribution of Instructional Faculty and Staff, by Whether They Have Retired from Another Position, and by Institution Type and Program Area: Fall 1998

Institution Type and Program Area	Percentage Retired from Another Position	
	Yes	No
All instructional faculty and staff in degree-granting institutions[1]	8.5	91.5
Public research	4.0	96.0
Private not-for-profit research	8.1	91.9
Public doctoral[2]	7.1	93.0
Private not-for-profit doctoral[2]	5.4	94.6
Public comprehensive	9.6	90.4
Private not-for-profit comprehensive	13.2	86.8
Private not-for-profit liberal arts	9.6	90.4
Public 2-year	10.3	89.7
Other[3]	8.5	91.5
Public institutions	8.0	92.0
Public 4-year doctoral institutions	5.0	95.0
Public 4-year nondoctoral institutions	9.1	90.9
Public 2-year institutions	10.3	89.7
Private not-for-profit institutions	9.7	90.3
Private 4-year doctoral institutions	7.0	93.0
Private 4-year nondoctoral institutions	11.1	88.9
Private 2-year institutions	8.5	91.5
All program areas	8.9	91.1
Agriculture/home economics	4.6	95.4
Business	11.8	88.2
Education	16.0	84.0
Engineering	12.0	88.1
Fine arts	6.0	94.0
Health sciences	6.7	93.3
Humanities	8.9	91.1
Natural sciences	8.5	91.6
Social sciences	6.9	93.1
All other fields	9.2	90.8

[1]All public and private, not-for-profit Title IV participating, degree-granting institutions in the fifty states and the District of Columbia.

[2]Includes institutions classified by the Carnegie Foundation as specialized medical schools and medical centers.

[3]Public liberal arts, private 2-year, and other specialized institutions except medical schools and medical centers.

Note: This table includes all full-time faculty (regardless of whether they had instructional responsibilities) and all other instructional staff. Percentages may not total to 100 because of rounding.

Source: U.S. Department of Education, National Center for Education Statistics, 1999 National Study of Postsecondary Faculty (NSOPF:99).

Conclusion

Political, social, and economic influences have altered the retirement process and created an environment of uncertainty for both individuals and institutions. The added flexibility now afforded faculty in an uncapped academic labor market presents institutions with both challenges and opportunities. Uncertainty characterizes the state of the current academic labor market with respect to retirement. However, there is no one single reason for this uncertainty. The aging of the population, elimination of mandatory retirement for tenured faculty, budget cutbacks, and general working conditions may be contributing factors. It is also becoming clear that faculty members have more choice about when and how to retire and that institutions appear to be experimenting with varied options to help accommodate these desires.

Elimination of mandatory retirement has clearly not had the worst-case impact on retirement patterns. Faculty still plan to retire conventionally in their mid-sixties on the whole. It does appear, though, that having the power to choose, faculty will increasingly vary in when and how they retire. Men and women appear to consider different factors. Faculty members at different types of institutions show different tendencies. The age and gender composition of individual disciplines appear to affect retirement patterns. But more clearly than any other factor than age, individual differences account for far more in the decision to retire than any measures of pay, workload, productivity, job satisfaction, or compensation. Accommodating those individual differences in intentional ways may have more impact on retirement flows than the elimination of mandatory retirement.

References

Atchley, R. C. *The Sociology of Retirement.* New York: Halsted Press, 1976.

Berger, A., Kirshstein, R., and Rowe, E. *Institutional Policies and Practices: Results from the 1999 National Study of Postsecondary Faculty, Institution Survey.* Washington, D.C.: National Center for Education Statistics, 2001.

Berry, L. H., Hammons, J. O., and Denny, G. S. "Faculty Retirement Turnover in Community Colleges: A Real or Imagined Problem?" *Community College Journal of Research and Practice,* 2001, 25(2), 123–136.

Chronister, J. L., Baldwin, R. G., and Conley, V. M. *Retirement and Other Departure Plans of Instructional Faculty and Staff in Higher Education Institutions.* Washington, D.C.: National Center for Education Statistics, 1997.

Chronister, J. L., and Kepple, T. R. *Incentive Early Retirement for Faculty: Innovative Responses to a Changing Environment.* Washington, D.C.: Association for the Study of Higher Education, 1987.

Clark, B. R. "Small Worlds, Different Worlds: The Uniqueness and Troubles of American Academic Professions." *Daedalus,* 1997, 126(4), 21–42.

Clark, R. L., and Hammond, P. B. (eds.). *To Retire or Not? Retirement Policy and Practice in Higher Education.* Philadelphia: University of Pennsylvania Press, 2001.

Conley, V. M. "Exploring Faculty Retirement Issues in Public Two-Year Institutions." *Journal of Applied Research in the Community College,* forthcoming.

Costa, D. L. *The Evolution of Retirement: An American Economic History, 1880–1990.* Chicago: University of Chicago Press, 1998.

Daniels, C. E., and Daniels, J. D. "College Faculty: The Retirement Decision and Retiree Health Benefits." *CUPA Journal,* 1992, *43*(1), 1–9.

Dey, E. L., Vander Putten, J. V., Han, S. W., and Coles, M. "Faculty Departure Plans: Differences Related to Institutional Type." Paper presented at the Thirty-Seventh Annual Forum of the Association for Institutional Research, Orlando, Fla., May 18–21, 1997.

Dorfman, L. T. "Stayers and Leavers: Professors in an Era of No Mandatory Retirement." *Educational Gerontology,* 2002, *28*(1), 15–33.

Ekerdt, D. J., DeViney, S., and Kosloski, K. "Profiling Plans for Retirement." *Journal of Gerontology,* 1996, *51B*(3), S140–S149.

Fogg, P. "Advancing in Age: As the Number of Old Professors at One University Increases, So Do the Challenges." *Chronicle of Higher Education,* June 3, 2005, p. A6.

Gray, K. *Retirement Plans and Expectations of TIAA-CREF Policyholders.* New York: Teachers Insurance and Annuity Association–College Retirement Equities Fund, 1989.

Gustman, A. L., and Steinmeir, T. L. "The Effects of Pensions and Retirement Policies on Retirement in Higher Education." *AEA Papers and Proceedings,* 1991, *81*(2), 111–115.

Hammond, P. B., and Morgan, H. P. (eds.). *Ending Mandatory Retirement for Tenured Faculty: The Consequences for Higher Education.* Washington, D.C.: National Academy Press, 1991.

Hanisch, K. A., and Hulin, C. L. "Job Attitudes and Organizational Withdrawal: An Examination of Retirement and Other Voluntary Withdrawal Behaviors." *Journal of Vocational Behavior,* 1990, *37*(1), 60–78.

Holden, K. C., and Hansen, W. L. (eds.). *The End of Mandatory Retirement: Effects on Higher Education.* New Directions for Higher Education, no. 65. San Francisco: Jossey-Bass, 1989.

Holden, K. C., and Hansen, W. L. "Reflections on an Earlier Study of Mandatory Retirement: What Came True and What We Can Still Learn." In R. L. Clark and P. B. Hammond (eds.), *To Retire or Not? Retirement Policy and Practice in Higher Education.* Philadelphia: University of Pennsylvania Press, 2001.

Keefe, J. "Intangible and Tangible Retirement Incentives." In R. L. Clark and P. B. Hammond, (eds.), *To Retire or Not? Retirement Policy and Practice in Higher Education.* Philadelphia: University of Pennsylvania Press, 2001.

Lewis, W. C. "Retirement Wealth, Income, and Decision Making in Higher Education." *Journal of Higher Education,* 1996, *67*(1), 85–102.

Lozier, G. G., and Dooris, M. J. *Faculty Retirement Projections Beyond 1994: Effects of Policy on Individual Choice.* Boulder, Colo.: Western Interstate Commission for Higher Education, 1991.

Monahan, D. J., and Greene, V. L. "Predictors of Early Retirement Among University Faculty." *Gerontologist,* 1987, *27*(1), 46–52.

Palmore, E. B. "Why Do People Retire?" *Aging and Human Development,* 1971, *2,* 269–283.

Patton, C. V. "Institutional Practices and Faculty Who Leave." In R. G. Baldwin and R. T. Blackburn, (eds.), *College Faculty: Versatile Human Resources in a Period of Constraint.* New Directions for Institutional Research, no. 40. San Francisco: Jossey-Bass, 1983.

Rees, A., and Smith, S. P. *Faculty Retirement in the Arts and Sciences.* Princeton, N.J.: Princeton University Press, 1991.

Rice, R. E., and Finkelstein, M. J. "The Senior Faculty: A Portrait and Literature Review." In M. J. Finkelstein and M. Lacelle-Peterson (eds.), *Developing Senior Faculty as Teachers.* New Directions for Teaching and Learning, no. 55. San Francisco: Jossey-Bass, 1993.

Ruhm, C. J. "Bridge Jobs and Partial Retirement." *Journal of Labor Economics,* 1990, 8(4), 482–501.

Smith, S. P. "Ending Mandatory Retirement in the Arts and Sciences." *American Economic Review,* 1991, 81(2), 106–110.

Szinovacz, M. E., and DeVincy, S. "Marital Characteristics and Retirement Decisions." *Research on Aging,* 2000, 22(5), 470–498.

U.S. Department of Education, National Center for Education Statistics. *1993 National Study of Postsecondary Faculty (NSOPF-93).* Washington, D.C.: U.S. Government Printing Office, 1993.

U.S. Department of Education, National Center for Education Statistics. *National Study of Postsecondary Faculty Institution Survey (NSOPF-99).* Washington, D.C.: U.S. Government Printing Office, 1999.

U.S. Department of Education, National Center for Education Statistics. *Data Analysis System.* Washington, D.C.: U.S. Government Printing Office, n.d. http://nces.ed.gov/dasol/.

Zimbler, L. J. *Background Characteristics, Work Activities, and Compensation of Faculty and Instructional Staff in Postsecondary Institutions: Fall 1998.* Washington, D.C.: National Center for Education Statistics, 2001.

VALERIE MARTIN CONLEY is assistant professor of higher education and associate director of the Center for Higher Education at Ohio University.

3

Phased retirement policies are more or less attractive financially and more or less accommodating of individual differences. They are also implemented in varying ways, variations that especially affect departments and academic programs.

Phased Retirement Policies

Natasha Janson

Policies providing for phased retirement for faculty have been in place for as many as thirty years or more. Historically, many colleges and universities allowed faculty to phase into retirement with reduced workloads (Chronister and Trainer, 1985). In some cases, individuals had fully retired and then agreed to teach a course or two at some agreed-on rate of pay. In other institutions, existing policies or individual agreements had allowed older faculty to renegotiate their work assignments to accommodate declining health or changing interests. In one case, the university's common practice was described this way: "We simply hired [retirees] back as adjuncts when departments needed them. We had no particular rules constraining or obliging either party. It was largely discretionary and informal." But the university realized it might be accused of age discrimination and needed rules because "there were a lot of individual deals before this policy, but this puts it all on a clearer footing." Another university shared a similar view of its own past practices: "In the past we negotiated individual retirement deals, sometimes giving too much to people we were happy to see go. This led to feelings of inequity and unfairness. So we instituted the phased policy to stop wheeling and dealing."

I am grateful to the Washington State University for granting me permission to include and review its phased retirement policy in this chapter. I am also grateful to faculty and administrators at diverse university campuses for their insights, some of which are quoted here.

NEW DIRECTIONS FOR HIGHER EDUCATION, no. 132, Winter 2005 © Wiley Periodicals, Inc.
Published online in Wiley InterScience (www.interscience.wiley.com) • DOI: 10.1002/he.195

The end of mandatory retirement in 1994 caused colleges and universities to worry that faculty would stay on the job indefinitely, creating a backlog of demand for new faculty. Phased retirement thus came to the forefront as a good option for enticing faculty with incentives to commit to a specific retirement date. About half of all colleges and universities offered early or phased retirement options as of the last national survey conducted in 1998, and in order to accommodate the expected numbers of individuals who might take phased retirement, it was clear that the more informal arrangements of the past needed to be revamped. These policies tended to be inconsistent from case to case (and therefore inequitable, as some departments were more generous than others). They also were sometimes inconsistent with the financial interests of either or both parties to the agreement, occasionally leaving individual faculty vulnerable to lower income from retirement plans or loss of benefits such as health insurance. Faculty, department chairs, or deans involved in these negotiations were not always sufficiently well informed (as is sometimes still the case) to provide constructively for the interests at stake.

Today phased retirement is more standardized, and attempts at equitability are created through formalized and written across-the-board policies that attempt to serve goals of both the institution and the individual. The phased retirement policy of Washington State University (WSU; see chapter appendix) shows how some institutions have devised and distributed such policies. In agreeing to the inclusion of its policy in this chapter, WSU has reminded us that individual institutions should assess their own particular contexts and needs when creating phased retirement policies. However, the elements and stipulations represented in WSU's policy are fairly typical of many phased retirement policies. Furthermore, the policy is sufficiently clear and well written that it can be held up as a model for the articulation of such policies.

Why Phased Retirement

In accepting phased retirement, faculty often agree to waive tenure rights and any claim to employment beyond a given date and negotiate a reduced workload for reduced pay. One interviewee offered this common explanation:

> The institution benefits from the policy by saving salary dollars and it gets people to commit to retirement. . . . The purpose of [our] policies is to provide an incentive to retire and to ease this difficult transition. Some people really can't just retire all at once. They need a phased process so they can go more slowly from full engagement to full retirement in gradual stages. The original purpose was economic, to [encourage] retirements after the uncapping. . . . It is, however, not a precision tool that weeds out those who should retire.

Policies provide an incentive for faculty to retire in a predictable and orderly way. These policies also help retain faculty with scarce expertise and help to preserve institutional memory where too much turnover would likely prove disruptive. These policies typically provide guidelines and frameworks within which retirement decisions can be made fairly and equitably across the institution. They provide a generous and humane vehicle to help faculty through a difficult adjustment after devoting their lives to a demanding profession. WSU's policy reads, "This Plan allows eligible personnel of the university to reduce their regular appointments to pursue personal or professional interests and to continue their academic and professional lives in gainful part-time employment. This Phased Retirement Plan provides an opportunity for individual career flexibility and forms an important part of the long-range personnel resource management of the University."

While many of those we interviewed affirmed the success of phased retirement policies at their institutions, they acknowledged that generally written policies had sometimes worked more as blunt instruments than as precisely targeted incentives. Individuals' retirement plans are affected by a variety of considerations: age, health, finances, and assorted issues of readiness. One view argues that standard terms and conditions are needed to prevent arbitrary deals. The other argues that individual faculty differ so substantially in their circumstances that negotiated individual treatment would help make phased retirement more attractive. This is the key challenge: striking the balance between across-the-board fairness and accommodating individual differences.

Reviewing the details of the policies helps to make clear some of the benefits as well as shortcomings of many of the phased retirement policies found on campuses today.

Elements of Phased Retirement Policies

Although faculty commonly retire in their mid-sixties, they generally report needing assurances that their fundamental interests in financial security and health insurance are protected, so the terms and conditions they are offered in phased retirement do affect their choices. We found that most phased retirement policies contained similar elements. The various elements of the policies can be understood in their entirety in the way that WSU has structured its phased retirement plan.

Terms of eligibility for phased retirement show a trend toward entitlement for all faculty meeting the years-of-service and age requirements. Some institutions do not categorically concede the right to phase in their policy, instead deferring the ultimate decision to a designated administrator. In many cases, the final decision is reserved for the institution's president. Many policies are worded in ways that protect the rights of both parties. WSU's policy reads: "Participation in the Phased Retirement Plan at Washington State University is voluntary and mutually agreeable to both the University and to employees of the University who participate in the WSU Retirement Plan (TIAA) and whose positions are reasonably able to be handled on a less than full-time basis without materially altering the expectations and responsibilities inherent in the position or title, and without adversely affecting the area or program, or the costs relating thereto."

Conversely, the minimum and maximum service and age eligibility for phased retirement programs are almost always explicitly stated, with most policies allowing faculty members at least by their mid-fifties and generally no older than their late sixties to opt for phased retirement, providing they have worked at the institution for at least ten to fifteen years, with some policies requiring as many as twenty.

Similarly, policies generally note the institution's agreement to continue to contribute to retirement, health, and life insurance plans during the phased retirement period, although the rate of contribution varies. For example, most of the phased retirement policies we reviewed declared that the institution would continue to contribute to retirement plans at the faculty member's full-time rate, although at least one policy stated that university contributions would be stopped when the faculty member entered phased retirement. WSU's policy allows that "the University will contribute to the retirement benefits program at the same percentage as when the participant was on a full-time salary." All of the policies reviewed asserted the right of phased retirees to draw from their retirement plan from the beginning of the phased retirement period. Health benefits and life insurance plans for the retirees and their dependents were usually continued as before the phased retirement period.

We reviewed the phased retirement policies provided by a diverse group of institutions and found that the terms and conditions for phased retirement covered the following similar topics.

Eligibility Requirements. Eligibility was usually based on a combination of age and years of service. For example, one policy established fifty-five as the minimum age of eligibility and required that an individual achieve some combination of age and years of service totaling to seventy-five. (Someone aged sixty, then, would have to have fifteen years of service to be eligible.) WSU's policy mandates that a faculty member be "55 years of age with at least 10 years of cumulative service to WSU."

Tenure Status. Eligibility for phased retirement was usually, although not always, conditioned on a waiver of tenure rights or on formal notice of retirement or intent to retire on a certain date. (But there are exceptions, as in the California State University System's and WSU's policy, that preserve tenure rights for those electing to phase.)

Notice. Eligibility to phase usually requires either notice of intent to retire at a certain time or a formal declaration of retirement. WSU requires that "several months ahead of the formal request, persons considering Washington State University's Phased Retirement Plan should informally discuss with their administrative unit head, the professional staff in Benefit Services, and other appropriate persons, the advantages and implications of a reduced appointment." A written request must then be submitted to the administrative head (for example, department chair). Pending U.S. Treasury Department regulations (2004) may affect the way notice of intent or notice of retirement will be used to determine eligibility to receive distributions from a retirement plan upon entering phased retirement.

Participation Period. Faculty members who choose the phased retirement option can expect to phase out within a fixed period. The policies most often set this period at between three and five years, with some negotiable variability for individual faculty. At the end of the specified period, the individual is not usually eligible for any further employment. (In a few cases, the phasing arrangement could continue, but this was not common. This was one element where WSU's policy appeared to be more anomalous, allowing phased retirement contracts of up to seven years.)

Work Assignment. Phased retirees are often technically assigned a set of responsibilities amounting to less than a full-time workload as customarily defined. The most common assignment was a 50 percent workload as defined by the institution. (An individual teaching four courses a term may be assigned to teach two courses on entering phased retirement.) In some cases, individuals with research projects or other duties had a commensurately reduced teaching assignment. Individuals usually have the option of working full time for a single semester or half time for two semesters. (We found that many prefer to work full time for one semester and take the other semester, plus the summer, off.) However, policies did differ, and sometimes significantly.

Salary. Pay for phased retirees was usually prorated: half pay for half time, for example. At WSU, the policy notes that "the written agreement . . . will specify the proportion of the phased retirement appointment, e.g.—50, 60, 75, 80 or 85 percent. . . . The salary during phased retirement is calculated at the appropriate percentage of the full-time base salary of the employee's position held just prior to entering phased retirement."

At some institutions, the rates of pay for the reduced appointments were slightly more complicated. Some offered a premium or balloon payment or retirement bonus, contingent on state laws, policies of retirement plan providers, and other considerations. For example, one institution's policy stated that phased retirees would work half time for 70 percent of their base salary at retirement, while another institution's policy allowed phased retirees to work up to 65 percent of full time earning a salary at the level of their appointment plus 10 percent. (Someone working half-time would receive 60 percent of their base pay.) At another institution, salaries were changed to lump-sum cash payouts of two times the average of the last three years of employment for faculty members who entered phased retirement.

Raises. Phased retirees were eligible for merit increases or supplemental pay for summer sessions under some plans but not under others. Some of those we interviewed complained that policies on raises for phased retirees were unclear. Lack of clarity about eligibility for raises often created tension between the retiree and the department.

Insurance. Premiums paid by the institution for health, life, and disability insurance were generally continued for the faculty member at the same rate as for full-time faculty. At least one institution, however, decreased the percentage of salary-based benefits paid in accordance with the phased retiree's reduced appointment. Someone who is employed at too small a fraction of full time may not be eligible for certain benefits. (Eligibility is often conditioned on some minimum level of work, such as the half-time requirement at WSU.)

Social Security and Pensions. Eligibility for retirement plan payouts and social security depend on the age of the individual, terms and conditions of the employment agreement, the structure of the retirement plan, and the individual's own relationship to these sources of income. The resulting financial implications may determine the degrees of freedom an individual has in electing (or not) to phase. WSU's policy advises that "those participants qualifying for Social Security retirement benefits may be eligible to draw those benefits while on phased retirement beginning at age 62 or any later date. In determining eligibility for benefits, the participant should consult a Social Security office."

Financial Planning. Financial planning for retirement was generally considered to be the individual's (and not the institution's) responsibility. However, one university covered services of a financial planner to help faculty understand the implications of their retirement options. WSU recommends that "in planning for income needs during phased retirement, it is important to review all sources of retirement income to determine eligibility for receiving payments, the taxability of the payments, and when it would be most advantageous to begin drawing these payments. This can be done with the assistance of University officials, TIAA-CREF representatives, or independent financial advisors."

Mutuality. Most policies specify that entry into phased retirement is contingent on the agreement of the institution and mutuality in working out the terms and conditions of the individual's assignment. At most institutions, the terms and conditions of an individual's assignment in phased retirement are negotiated at the department level, while the pay, benefits, and length of the arrangement are specified at the institutional level. This generally allows departments and individuals to play to each other's needs and strengths, while preserving the overall equity of treatment among departments.

While department chairs are usually in the best position to achieve mutuality with the individual faculty member, substantive reviews at higher levels are needed to ensure equity across all departments. At WSU, there is an application process: "The University employee wishing to participate in the Phased Retirement Plan will submit a request, in writing, to the department chair and/or other administrative head. The written request should include no less than the desired percent of effort, the desired effective date and duration of the phased retirement, and an explanation of why this desired reduced effort and phased retirement would not materially alter the expectations and responsibilities inherent in the position." The application process is followed by an approval process in which approval is required by the requisite chain of command, from the department head, to the dean, to the vice president. More about the negotiation of the phased retirement agreement is included in the next section.

Implementing Phased Retirement Policies

Phased retirement policies are variably successful in proportion to how they are executed. The most important issues reported by those we interviewed were related to how negotiations with individual faculty over the terms of phased retirement affected the individual's department.

At most institutions, the terms and conditions of an individual's assignment in phased retirement are negotiated at the department level, while the pay, benefits, and length of the arrangement are specified at the institutional level.

At most of the institutions we visited, the candor and clarity of the specific terms and conditions of the phased retirement assignment as negotiated between individual and department chair were instrumental to the overall net effects of the phased retirement agreement for the faculty member and the institution. As one administrator said, "Agreements [which must be in writing] are negotiated with individuals by department chairs. Chairs know what the dean wants these assignments to look like, but they have the flexibility to negotiate individually on things like research and advising, which are important in some cases. They try to blend individual faculty needs with the interests of the department."

Central administration also was sometimes seen to work to facilitate these frontline negotiations. One individual could not afford the usual terms of phased retirement under the institution's existing policy. This faculty member noted the high cost of health care for an adult dependent with special needs, costs that would continue indefinitely. The university, in approving a phased retirement plan for this individual, made provisions well beyond the usual: to continue health coverage for the rest of the dependent's life.

Exceptions aside, central administrators or deans almost always supported the need for formalized policy norms and standards that would ensure equity and fairness. Among other reasons cited, chairs tend to be accommodating in these negotiations. Sometimes they are helping colleagues of long standing and feel they cannot take a tough line. As one administrator noted, "I don't know of any chair who has said no to a request to phase."

However, standardized policies can sometimes mitigate the flexibility that departments try to achieve. As one relatively new chair said, "In this department, we wanted the phase period to be only three years and attempted to negotiate that with two individuals. They preferred five years, and got the central administration to back them up. So, effectively, the five-year eligibility period is now (in practice) a right rather than a negotiable maximum."

Policy-Framing Issues

There is some debate over whether the terms and conditions of phased retirement policies are clearly framed, clearly explained, and consistently administered. What follows are some of the critical policy-framing issues raised by both faculty and administrators during our interviews.

Contracts. Most institutions specified that phased retirement policies were to be governed by written contracts. At WSU, for example, the policy states, "A written agreement setting forth mutually agreeable terms and conditions of an individual's phased retirement arrangement will be signed by the participant and the authorized Vice President. It will contain the following elements [it then lists those elements]." In two institutions, however, we found that the arrangement was not governed by any written agreement. One of our interviewees said he expected to continue his research after leaving the phased program; he said that he understood the three-year agreement was firm but that he had not signed anything binding to this effect: "There was no contract." Whether he will want to extend employment may be an open question, but he spoke as if there were ways he could somehow extend his employment, perhaps with a grant. Another pointed out, "I only signed a letter of intent, which I don't think is legally binding on either me or the university."

The rights of the individual and the rights of the institution were unclear in these cases. In fact, neither party might be able to enforce the terms and conditions they assumed to be in effect. Without a clear contractual arrangement, both put their interests at risk.

Salary and Benefits. Individual faculty are most concerned about their cash flow in the phased retirement period. Some are positioned to accept half pay for half-time work. Some have no choice, by reason of a medical condition that precludes full-time employment or because they are simply worn out and no longer feel they can sustain a full load. Others need a combination of half-time pay, retirement income, and social security. A decision about whether to phase may well turn on whether an individual feels he or she can afford it. Depending on the source of retirement pay, individuals may not be able to earn more than a given fraction of their pre-retirement pay and still be able to draw on their retirement accounts. In other cases, they are barred from drawing on their retirement accounts for one of several reasons. Most commonly, they are employed (or paid) at too great a fraction of their previous arrangement. Individuals who have had twelve-month contracts may or may not be eligible to continue their full-year employment. Cutting back from a twelve-month base to nine months, and at 50 percent of that, represents a larger cut in cash flow than some individuals have been willing to accept.

The ability of those who phase to draw on retirement pensions or annuities may be affected by pending Internal Revenue Service regulations. As proposed in late 2004, these regulations would require that individuals formally retire without an agreement to continue any form of employment by their institutions in order to be eligible for retirement payouts.

Faculty Rights. There is general agreement that phasing should be a matter of the faculty member's personal choice. Electing to phase should be free of any pressure and should be a matter of both individual choice and departments' ability to accommodate needs. One institution emphasized the need to inform eligible faculty of its policies: "We try to inform them of the policy, but most don't know about it. We write faculty over 60 to let them know it is an option. The terms are flexible and are negotiated at the level of department chairs." Chairs at another institution emphasized the need to let individuals decide if they wanted to take advantage of the option: "The institution should stay neutral as to whether any individual should elect it. Neither push nor withhold the program. Negotiate in good faith with individuals." But phased retirees' eligibility to apply for research grants, travel funds, sabbatical leaves, promotion, or faculty development funds are arenas in which misunderstandings can occur. At WSU, specific mention is made of the tuition remission (continued as when full time) and sabbatical policies (restricted to full-time employees) under phased retirement.

Another particularly ambiguous area is that of grant funding, which is more problematic at the later stages of phased retirement. Individuals sometimes want to keep their grants and projects alive beyond the date at which they have formally agreed to terminate their employment.

Faculty Responsibilities. Accounting for time and performance were concerns at several institutions. In one case, a provost felt the policy at his or her institution was too vague on conditions that would lead to terminating the employment of a phased retiree whose performance was considered inadequate. Administrators noted that it was difficult to keep track of phased retirees and their time on the job. WSU's policy did note, "The participant continues to operate under the stipulations of the appropriate

[Faculty and Administrative Professional] Handbook, except as otherwise provided in this policy."

Phased retirees are also usually able to walk away from the agreement at any point without penalty. Institutions cannot always depend on them to finish the full term of (usually) five years or even to give advance notice when they decide to leave altogether.

Individuals whose assignment is either primarily in research or substantially so present first-line supervisors with special challenges. WSU's policy recognizes that "for the purpose of a faculty phased retirement contract, the department chair and dean will consider non-teaching duties as well as courses taught in defining a full-time faculty load and percentages thereof. In developing the provisions of the contract, the academic participant and the Dean or other administrative unit head may negotiate the type and amount of non-teaching assignment expected of the participant, consistent with the reduced assignment."

Phased retirees with primarily research- or service-oriented duties may be working off campus and at irregular hours. One retired dean we interviewed understood how difficult it was for his successor to account for faculty time, so he voluntarily kept a log of actual hours worked and activities in which he engaged during those times. He submitted his log to the dean's office monthly but reported that the logs had never been acknowledged or, as nearly as he could tell, even read. At one comprehensive university, it was felt that some phased retirees had succeeded in negotiating research assignments for themselves that exceeded the norm for their institution, presenting both equity and supervisory issues that had not been resolved.

Departmental Logistics. Negotiations at the departmental level may be complicated by the logistical implications of office space, lab space, and support services that must be rearranged when a faculty member phases. These issues are not usually covered in policies on phased retirement and become negotiable between eligible faculty and their department chairs or deans. In some situations, departments badly need the space for new faculty or new projects, but phased retirees feel entitled to keep it. Few are happy to find themselves sharing an office or giving up their labs and research assistants, but this is often the fulcrum that institutions need to pry scarce resources loose to support the new generation of faculty. WSU's policy explains that "required office, laboratory space, secretarial service, computer use, and other support services may be made available. These services will be negotiable in developing the provisions of the contract. The university's intent is to provide appropriate laboratory and office space, but exigencies of space and facilities use may not always permit this."

Permanent versus One-Time Policies. We found that some institutions had experimented with various retirement incentive offers. In some cases, these offers were made for limited periods, so that an eligible faculty member would have to elect or forgo the option, such as the opportunity to phase or to receive a bonus payment upon full retirement. Because the golden parachute options were not always popular, some institutions reoffered more attractive packages within a fairly short time period. These recycled incentive programs ultimately became self-defeating because faculty began to sense that a better offer would follow. Consequently, they were more inclined to put retirement off to see if they might benefit more from a subsequent program.

In a few cases, institutional leaders felt they had rushed into (or been rushed into) providing incentives to encourage retirements. Although there was certainly reason for concern with the abolition of mandatory retirement, it now appears in hindsight that those concerns were unrealistic because NSOPF:99 data show that faculty typically plan to retire in their mid-sixties on the average regardless of incentives offered by institutions. With this experience in mind, institutions might consider stabilizing policies to help individual faculty foresee (well in advance) terms and conditions under which they can plan to retire in a more predictable way.

Conclusion

Phased retirement policies appear to be relatively simple and their implementation appears to be straightforward. Standardized institutional phased retirement policies regarding pay, benefits, and length of service provide equity in granting phased retirements to individuals across the institution. Frontline negotiations between the faculty member and the department chair regarding work assignments and expected logistical support provide the flexibility often needed for the success of these arrangements. Communication among all the parties—that is, well-articulated and written institutional phased retirement policies such as WSU's—as well as verbal and written communication between phased retirees and department chairs, is critical to satisfactory implementation of the policies. Most institutions, departments, and faculty members express satisfaction with phased retirement when the basic needs of each are fulfilled. For institutions, this means that policies provide structured ways to predict retirements (for example, with articulated length-of-service agreements). For departments, this means policies are articulated such that departments have some voice in how many individuals phase at a time and in arranging mutually beneficial work assignments (for example, having the phased retiree teach a survey course). And for individuals who are able to meet their basic security needs through phased retirement policies and also know exactly what is expected of them and what they can expect, the opportunity to phase into retirement has been noted to be particularly beneficial and satisfactory.

Appendix: Washington State University Phased Retirement Policy

Washington State University Phased Retirement Plan is a program designed to give University employees—faculty and administrative professional staff who participate in the WSU-Retirement Plan—an opportunity for pre-retirement reduction of full-time service while gradually phasing into retirement over a period of years. This Plan allows eligible personnel of the university to reduce their regular appointments to pursue personal or professional interests and to continue their academic and professional lives in gainful part-time employment. This Phased Retirement Plan provides an opportunity for individual career flexibility and forms an important part of the long-range personnel resource management of the University.

The Phased Retirement Plan is flexible and enables participants to have income for current financial needs—through part-time salary, retirement annuity payments, and other sources of income made possible because of the workload reduction—while allowing them to accrue additional retirement benefits that are paid upon full retirement. In planning for income needs during phased retirement, it is important to review all sources of retirement income to determine eligibility for receiving payments, the taxability of the payments, and when it would be most advantageous to begin drawing these payments. This can be done with the assistance of University officials, TIAA-CREF representatives, or independent financial advisors. Participants who retain appointments for greater than or equal to 50 percent time continue to be eligible for applicable employee benefits, including health insurance.

Phased retirement is intended to support the University's excellence. It permits the University to retain the services and contributions of senior faculty and administrative professional staff while enabling participants to continue to remain in their profession and to build additional financial security for the future. The Plan also assists in diversifying the University's work force by releasing positions and funds that can contribute to renewing its personnel resources by filling vacancies with new, diverse employees.

The WSU Phased Retirement Plan is a voluntary and mutually agreed upon arrangement between the University and the participant. At any time, upon request by the President, the Plan may be reviewed and modified without affecting already existing contracts.

The President may report periodically to the Board of Regents on the academic, personnel, and fiscal impact of the Phased Retirement Plan.

All information presented in this plan must remain aligned to legislation, laws, rules and regulations from federal, state, local and institutional governance. This Plan is subject to change in order to maintain compliance with both Internal Revenue Service and Social Security Administration rules.

Source: http://www.wsu.edu/benefits/retirementinfo/phasedRetPolicy.ht

NEW DIRECTIONS FOR HIGHER EDUCATION • DOI 10.1002/he

Eligibility Criteria for Application to Participate. Participation in the Phased Retirement Plan at Washington State University is voluntary and mutually agreeable to both the University and to employees of the University who participate in the WSU Retirement Plan (TIAA) and whose positions are reasonably able to be handled on a less than full-time basis without materially altering the expectations and responsibilities inherent in the position or title, and without adversely affecting the area or program, or the costs relating thereto.

Criteria for participation in the plan, including the above, are as follows:

Status: At least 50% permanent employment with Washington State University

Service: 55 years of age with at least 10 years of cumulative service to WSU

Position: Holding a position that is reasonably able to be handled on a less than full-time basis without materially altering the expectations and responsibilities inherent in the position or title, and without adversely affecting the area or program, or the cost relating thereto.

Budget: Funds allocated to position held by incumbent

Academic Impact: No detrimental impact to Washington State University programs/students

Contract. A written agreement setting forth mutually agreeable terms and conditions of an individual's phased retirement arrangement will be signed by the participant and the authorized Vice President. It will contain the following elements:

Length of Contract. Phased retirement contracts for half-time service or more are typically limited to seven years. Extensions may be renewed on a year by year basis.

Phased retirement contracts are not available for less than half-time service.

Reduction in Time-Base. The written agreement will indicate the effective date of entry into the program. It will specify the proportion of the phased retirement appointment, e.g., 50, 60, 75, 80 or 85 percent. All reductions must be approved in writing by the appropriate administrative unit head before being presented to the authorized Vice President.

It is possible to either periodically reduce the percent of effort, or initially reduce the effort to a certain percent and remain at that percent of effort until full retirement.

The percent of effort may not be increased except in unusual circumstances and only with the written support by the administrative unit head and approval of the authorized Vice President.

Contingency Clause. The initial arrangement for a reduction in time-base is contingent upon budgetary feasibility as determined in the annual budget preparation immediately prior to the effective date of the contract and may be reviewed annually.

Salary. The salary during phased retirement is calculated at the appropriate percentage of the full-time base salary of the employee's position held just prior to entering phased retirement. The participant may receive periodic salary increments provided these increments follow current Washington State University policy.

Employee Benefits

Retirement Plan. Participants in the phased retirement plan remain eligible for the University's percentage contribution to the pension plan. The University will contribute to the retirement benefits program at the same percentage as when the participant was on a full-time salary.

Example: An employee decided to participate in the phased retirement plan at a 50% appointment.

Regular salary: $60,000
Reduced salary: $30,000
University Contribution (based on 10% contribution rate): 10% × $30,000 = $3,000. Employee contribution matches employer contribution, required via payroll reduction.

Health and Life Insurance. Participants with appointments of 50% or greater will continue to receive the University's regular contributions toward health, optical, dental and life insurance plans as per all full-time employees.

Employee contributions towards disability plans may continue but benefits will be based upon the participant's reduced salary.

Social Security. Those participants qualifying for Social Security retirement benefits may be eligible to draw those benefits while on phased retirement beginning at age 62 or any later date. In determining eligibility for benefits, the participant should consult a Social Security office.

Tuition Remission Benefits. The participant continues to enjoy tuition remission benefits in accordance with current Washington State University policy for full-time employees.

Vacation and Sick Leave. For those appointees on phased retirement with titles that accrue sick leave and/or vacation leave credit, those benefits continue under the same pro rata conditions as for permanent part-time employees.

Sabbaticals and Leaves of Absence. Participants in the Phased Retirement Plan are not eligible for sabbaticals since that benefit is available only to full-time employees.

Participants in the Phased Retirement Plan are eligible to participate in shared leave and FMLA leave in the same pro rata conditions as for permanent part-time employees.

University Status of Participant

Tenure. A tenured faculty member who participates in the Phased Retirement Plan shall continue to be deemed a tenured member of the faculty for the specific length of time indicated in the phased retirement agreement.

Promotion. The academic participant remains eligible for consideration for promotion. Such advancements shall be assessed on the same basis as for full-time appointees.

Faculty Senate Voting Privileges. Voting privileges are subject to the rules and regulations of the bylaws and constitution of the Faculty Senate.

Non-Teaching Assignments. For the purpose of a faculty phased retirement contract, the department chair and dean will consider non-teaching duties as well as courses taught in defining a full-time faculty load and percentages thereof. In developing the provisions of the contract, the academic participant and the Dean or other administrative unit head may negotiate the type and amount of non-teaching assignment expected of the participant, consistent with the reduced assignment.

Space and Support Requirements. Required office, laboratory space, secretarial service, computer use, and other support services may be made available. These services will be negotiable in developing the provisions of the contract.

The University's intent is to provide appropriate laboratory and office space, but exigencies of space and facilities use may not always permit this.

Faculty and Administrative Professional Handbooks. The participant continues to operate under the stipulations of the appropriate Handbook, except as otherwise provided in this policy.

Procedures

Preliminary Process. Several months ahead of the formal request, persons considering Washington State University's Phased Retirement Plan should informally discuss with their administrative unit head, the professional staff in Benefit Services, and other appropriate persons, the advantages and implications of a reduced appointment.

Application Process. The University employee wishing to participate in the Phased Retirement Plan will submit a request, in writing, to the department chair and/or other administrative head. The written request should include no less than the desired percent of effort, the desired effective date and duration of the phased retirement, and an explanation of why this desired reduced effort and phased retirement would not materially alter the expectations and responsibilities inherent in the position.

Approval Process. The department chair or other administrative unit head will consult with the applicant and other appropriate members of the department to evaluate requests in terms of planning, personnel needs, phased retirement plan costs, space and support requirements for the applicant and potential replacement(s), and other pertinent factors.

1. The chair or other administrative head will submit a report of the unit recommendation and a preliminary listing of the proposed contract terms to the Dean or other administrative officer. The applicant will receive a copy of this recommendation.
2. The Dean or administrative officer will review the proposed contract terms and the departmental or unit recommendation and will forward it, together with a personal recommendation, to the appropriate Vice President. The applicant will receive a copy of this recommendation.
3. The Vice President will make a determination based on the facts and merits of the recommendations. The Vice President's decision is final. Only the Vice President may authorize exception to the provisions of the Phased Retirement Plan. Any exception to the policy must be in writing and signed by both parties.

Development of the Formal Contract. If the request is approved by the authorized Vice President, the applicant will meet with the Vice President for Business Affairs or his/her designee to draw up a formal contract that will contain the provisions specified in this policy. Washington State University Legal Counsel will review all contracts.

References

Chronister, J. L., and Trainer, A. "Early, Partial, and Phased Retirement Programs in Public Higher Education: A Report on Institutional Experiences." *Journal of the College and University Personnel Association,* 1985, 36(4), 27–31.

U.S. Treasury Department. *Distributions from a Pension Plan under a Phased Retirement Program: Notice of Proposed Rulemaking.* Washington, D.C.: U. S. Treasury Department, 2004. http://www.treas.gov/press/releases/reports/js2094_111004phasedretirementreg.pdf.

NATASHA JANSON is a graduate student and research assistant at the College of William and Mary.

4

The implications of the policy choices made in setting up a phased retirement system are demonstrated by its variety of outcomes.

Managing a Phased Retirement Program: The Case of UNC

Steven G. Allen, Robert L. Clark, Linda S. Ghent

Colleges and universities are facing a series of challenges as they attempt to achieve their educational objectives. A primary concern of every institution is the need to recruit and retain quality faculty with the skills necessary to provide the level of teaching and research associated with the mission of the university. Faculties are aging, mandatory retirement has been eliminated, health care costs are soaring, and budgets are growing slowly, if at all. In this environment, many institutions have reconsidered their retirement policies in conjunction with other employment and compensation policies as a means of developing a faculty that will meet the demands of the twenty-first century (Clark, 2005). In an effort to alter retirement decisions and achieve the desired size and age composition of their faculty, universities have implemented early and phased retirement plans, revised retiree health plans, and moved toward a greater reliance on contract faculty (Clark and Ma, 2005).

This analysis focuses on the use of formal phased retirement plans by universities. We begin by describing phased retirement plans and how they are implemented. Next, we examine the managerial objectives of these programs, what types of workers are most likely to accept early retirement, and how these programs influence the timing of retirement. We end with a case study of the phased retirement plan at the University of North Carolina (UNC). This discussion describes the results of a statistical analysis of the changes in the retirement patterns of the faculty at UNC after the introduction of phased retirement. There are relatively few studies of phased retirement plans;

however, existing surveys and research (for example, Allen 2005; Leslie and Janson, 2005; Ghent, Allen, and Clark, 2001) indicate that these plans are popular with faculty and provide value to institutions.

What Is Phased Retirement?

Universities have often rehired retired professors to teach an occasional class. Typically these reemployment contracts were short term (one semester or one year) and would pay the professor only a small percentage of his or her previous salary. Such reemployment was on an as-needed basis as identified by the university. Thus, the on-campus employment options available to typical older faculty members were to keep working full time as a tenured professor or retire completely, with the possibility that the university might reemploy them at a substantially lower part-time salary.

Formal phased retirement programs are much different. Although the characteristics of these programs vary across institutions, certain common attributes define formal phased retirement plans. In general, these plans specify part-time work for part-time pay. A typical program would be half-time work for half-time pay. If a university wanted to encourage greater participation in the plan, the terms could be more generous, such as half-time work for three-quarters pay. Compensation is directly linked to pre-retirement earnings. Formal phased retirement plans should be considered the final stage of a lifetime contract between the tenured professor and the university.

Enrollment in phased retirement plans is usually at the choice of the faculty member, although some universities may limit the total number of phased retirees if it is believed that an excess of phased retirees will have an adverse impact on educational quality. Prior to entering phased retirement, an applicant must negotiate what will constitute part-time employment. In most cases, the faculty member and his or her department chair or dean will develop a new part-time workload with specific assignments for the phased retirement period. In general, these negotiations will result in the professor's teaching half of his or her preretirement teaching load. However, some contracts could have the phased retiree engaged in more advising or directing undergraduate or graduate programs, or all of the person's time could be devoted to research. Optimally the negotiations would yield specific assignments that add value to the university and are consistent with the talents and preferences of the faculty member.

Phased retirement plans provide older faculty with a new employment choice. Instead of full-time work on campus or complete retirement, the eligible faculty member can select a part-time employment option. Enrollment in a phased retirement program generally requires faculty to relinquish tenure at the time of enrollment or at a specified future date. In exchange for giving up tenure, the faculty member receives an employment contract for a fixed duration at a specified salary. Phased retirement contracts vary in length but usually run for three to five years.

Most phased retirement plans have specified eligibility conditions based on age and years of service; for example, eligibility criteria could be age fifty with twenty years of service or age sixty with five years of service. Most plans are limited to tenured faculty. Thus, phased retirement is offered to senior faculty who have provided long service to the university in exchange for a commitment to retire at a specified date and relinquish their lifetime tenure.

In developing a phased retirement plan, one must consider how the move from full-time work to part-time employment will affect retirement benefits. Several important issues must be considered. If the faculty member is a participant in a defined benefit plan, a dominant consideration is how the decline in earnings during phased retirement will affect current and future pension benefits. If the phased retiree continues to be considered a regular faculty member and these years of reduced earnings are used to calculate future pension benefits, entry into phased retirement could result in a substantial reduction in future retirement benefits since final average salary would be lower. The typical formula in a defined benefit plan calculates retirement benefits by multiplying a generosity parameter (say 1.5 percent per year of service) times the number of years of employment times the final average salary of the worker. In general, plans include the last or highest three to five years of earnings in the averaging period. Thus, if a person enters phased retirement and these reduced earnings are included in the determination of the salary average used to calculate benefits, phased retirement would result in much lower retirement benefits.

As a result, phased retirement will not be a very attractive option for faculty who are enrolled in a defined benefit pension plan. However, if the phased retiree is considered to be a retiree and his or her annual pension benefit is already determined when entering phased retirement, then the combination of half-time earnings and a full pension benefit can be a very attractive level of income as the professor moves toward complete retirement.

For participants in defined contribution plans, the decision to enter phased retirement should be made in conjunction with available choices about full or partial annuitization of pension assets. The phased retiree may want to smooth the stream of annual income by having a smaller annual pension during phased retirement and then increasing the pension payments when earnings stop at the end of phased retirement. The flexibility of payout options in defined contribution plans makes them an attractive option for persons considering phased retirement. The existence of phased retirement options will increase the need for faculty to have a better understanding of their retirement plans and the income that they can expect in retirement. (Clark and d'Ambrosio, 2003, discuss the importance of financial literacy and responses to financial education programs.)

**Table 4.1. Percentage of Universities Offering Phased
Retirement Plans**

Category	Private	Public	Total
Research and Doctoral Institutions	50%	31%	35%
Master's Institutions	38%	23%	29%
Baccalaureate Institutions	30%	24%	29%
All Colleges and Universities	35%	26%	30%

Entries indicate the percentage of universities in each category that had a phased retirement plan.
Source: Ronald Ehrenberg, 2003. "Survey of Changes in Faculty Retirement Plans." http://www.
aaup.org/Issues/retirement/retirepg.htm.

During recent years, phased retirement programs have been adopted by
many colleges and universities. Phased retirement plans are also being intro-
duced by firms outside the educational sector of the economy as these employers also attempt to revise their retirement programs in the face of a changing
labor market (Clark and Rappaport, 2001). However, a study by Watson
Wyatt, 1999, found that academic employers were much more likely to adopt
phased retirement plans than firms in other sectors. Table 4.1 shows the incidence of phased retirement plans from the Survey of Changes in Faculty
Retirement Policies (Ehrenberg, 2003). This survey reported that in 2000, 30
percent of responding institutions had established phased retirement plans.
These plans were most commonly adopted by private colleges and universities (35 percent). Among all categories of institutions, research and doctoral
universities had a higher incidence of phased retirement plans (35 percent).
Not coincidently, private research universities have been most concerned
about the impact of ending mandatory retirement and the aging of their faculties. Half of all private, research, and doctoral institutions had established
formal phased retirement plans. The trend toward greater use of phased programs seems to be continuing. Leslie and Janson (2005) report that approximately half of all institutions of higher education have now adopted these
plans. Although more and more colleges and universities are adopting them,
their introduction does not always occur with debate. Switkes (2005) provides
a review of the development of such a plan and the debate over its implementation at the University of California.

Managing Phased Retirement Programs

Universities adopt phased retirement plans as part of their faculty retirement
policies. These plans should be used in conjunction with the institution's
basic retirement plan, any retiree health plans, and any other retirement
plans offered by the university. The primary objectives of academic administrators in adopting phased retirement plans are to facilitate the orderly

retirement of senior faculty, address the aging of the faculty, and provide a new employment benefit to faculty. Phased retirement may encourage some faculty to move from full-time work to part-time work without tenure, while others may choose part-time work over complete retirement.

Let us consider the costs and benefits of phased retirement plans from the standpoint of the university. The direct cost of phased retirement plans can be minimal. If phased retirees are paid half of their annual salary for a half-time workload, these programs can be essentially cost neutral. Key cost considerations include whether the university continues to provide other benefits, such as pension contributions and health insurance, and how these benefits are financed. In some plans, the faculty member retires, gives up tenure, and then enters phased retirement. In other plans, the professor specifies a future retirement date but remains a tenured faculty member who is working part time until the agreed-on date. In the first case, employment benefits often end, and the phased retiree is treated as a retiree. In the second case, the phased retiree is treated as a worker, and most benefits would continue. Some plans allow pension contributions to continue, and the amount may be based on the previous full-time salary.

Indirect costs of phased retirement plans tend to be related to concerns over performance and management of phased retirees. Key questions include whether the phased retiree will continue to perform his or her duties at an acceptable level and whether the department will be able to continue to provide appropriate educational services while the person is in phased retirement. Deans and department chairs often worry about how the reduction in labor cost associated with a phased retiree will be used. For example, will the funds be returned to the department of the phased retiree, or will they be reallocated for other purposes? (Allen, 2005, and Leslie and Janson, 2005, discuss the results of surveys of academic administrators and their concerns over the adoption of phased retirement plans.)

Another consideration for academic administrators is which faculty will enter phased retirement and whether phased retirement will prolong or truncate faculty work life. Several possible scenarios exist, and some of these possibilities are more desirable to the institution than others. (Allen, Clark, and Ghent, 2004, provide a formal model of work and retirement decisions of older faculty in the presence of a phased retirement plan.) First, quality faculty may choose to enter phased retirement rather than continuing to work full time. This may result in the university's losing a valuable resource sooner than expected. Second, quality faculty may choose to enter phased retirement rather than retiring completely. Thus, the university may retain a valuable resource for longer than expected. Third, a faculty member who is not producing at a high level may choose to enter phased retirement rather than remain on the job full time. This provides desired turnover and specific information on when the faculty member would completely retire. Finally, a faculty member who is not producing at a high level may choose to enter phased retirement rather than retire completely. In this case, the low-quality faculty member may remain somewhat longer than otherwise, but the university now knows when the individual will completely leave the institution.

It is difficult to know which of these cases might dominate in a particular institution. To address this question, the next section presents the results of a case study of UNC. However, it seems clear that phased retirement plans have the potential of being a win-win situation for senior faculty and their universities. Senior professors can select an alternative transition from full-time work to complete retirement that better fits their preferences and income needs. Faculty gain because these plans represent a new employment option and tend to be voluntary. Universities gain information about the retirement plans of their faculty and achieve greater flexibility in their human resource planning without incurring significant new costs.

Phased Retirement at the University of North Carolina

In 1998, the UNC board of governors adopted a five-year trial phased retirement program. (Detailed descriptions of the adoption of this phased retirement plan by UNC and its characteristics are found in Ghent, Allen, and Clark, 2001; Allen, Clark, and Ghent, 2004; and Allen, 2005. Interested readers can examine the details of the phased retirement program at North Carolina State University by going to http://www.ncsu.edu/provost/offices/academic_personnnel/policy/prp_guidelines.html.) The board required each of the fifteen degree-granting campuses to establish a phased retirement plan that met certain basic characteristics. The phased retirement program provides half-time pay for half-time work. Faculty entering into phased retirement had to resign and give up tenure before enrolling in the program. Individuals had to be at least age fifty with twenty years of service or age sixty with five years of service at the same institution. Each campus was allowed to select the length of the phased retirement contract between one and five years. Twelve of the campuses chose a three-year program, two chose a two-year plan, and one opted for a five-year phased retirement program. After a five-year review of the experimental program, the board of governors adopted the phased retirement plan as a permanent employment benefit for UNC faculty.

Eligible faculty negotiate their new job assignments with their department chair. The phased retiree can work full time one semester and be off the second semester, or the faculty member can work half time each semester. Phased retirees do not receive any employee benefits; however, UNC has a retiree health plan that provides the same health insurance to retirees as that received by active workers. Thus, phased retirees receive the same health insurance coverage as when they were employed as active faculty.

Table 4.2. Retirement Rates for University of North Carolina Faculty

Year	Full Retirement	Phased Retirement	Sum
1994–1995	8.7		8.7
1995–1996	8.7		8.7
1996–1997	8.8		8.8
Average before phased retirement	8.7		8.7
1997–1998	7.3	3.5	10.8
1998–1999	8.0	2.3	10.3
1999–2000	7.0	3.9	10.9
2000–2001	6.1	3.4	9.5
2001–2002	7.3	2.2	9.5
2002–2003	3.8	2.5	6.3
Average after phased retirement	6.6	3.0	9.6
Change in retirement rate after phased retirement	−2.1	3.0	0.9

Source: Annual census of faculty employment, UNC system.

Entering phased retirement is at the option of the individual faculty member who meets the eligibility criteria. Departments have the right to place caps on the maximum number of faculty who could be in phased retirement at any one time.

Table 4.2 reports the retirement rates for all faculty meeting the eligibility conditions for entrance into phased retirement for three years before the introduction of phased retirement (1994 to 1997) and for six years after the adoption of phased retirement. (The retirement rate for any pair of years, for example, 1994–1995, equals the percentage of those employed in the first year who are no longer employed in the second year.) Prior to the introduction of phased retirement, full retirement rates averaged 8.7 percent of eligible faculty per year. This means that fewer than one in ten faculty who were age fifty or older with twenty years of service (or age sixty or older with five years of service) left the university each year. In the first five years after the adoption of the phased retirement plan, the total retirement rate (full retirement plus phased retirement) averaged 10.2 percent of eligible faculty. During this period, the full retirement rate declined to 7.1 percent, and the phased retirement rate averaged 3.1 percent. In 2002–2003, the full retirement rate dropped sharply to 3.8 percent from the 7.3 percent that prevailed in 2001–2002. The decline in the full retirement rate occurred in the presence of adverse economic conditions and a sharp decline in the stock market. However, the phased retirement rate increased slightly from 2.2 percent in 2001–2002 to 2.5 percent in 2002–2003.

These data indicate that phased retirement was a popular option among UNC faculty. Over the entire period, phased retirees represented 31 percent of all persons retiring from the university. In other words, one out of every

NEW DIRECTIONS FOR HIGHER EDUCATION • DOI 10.1002/he

three persons who retired from the university entered phased retirement, while the other two retired completely.

The data imply that a substantial portion of phased retirees were individuals who would have remained on the job full time if phased retirement had not been an option. In a survey of phased retirees conducted in fall 2003, Allen (2005) found that 84 percent of the respondents said they would have continued working full time if the option of phased retirement had not been available. On average, the survey respondents said they would have worked an additional 3.6 years in the absence of phased retirement.

Ghent, Allen, and Clark (2001) provide more rigorous econometric evidence indicating that most phased retirees would have continued working full time if the program had not been available. The available evidence indicates that phased retirement increased total retirements (full plus phased) among senior faculty. At the same time, the full retirement rate declined by about two percentage points, indicating that some faculty who otherwise would have retired completely also chose to enter phased retirement.

Determinants of Changes in Retirement Behavior

Academic administrators considering the adoption of phased retirement plans should be interested in determining what personal and institutional factors affect faculty decisions to accept phased retirement. To identify the determinants of participation in phased retirement plans, we examined retirement rates at UNC before and after the introduction of the phased retirement plan. Data from faculty censuses from the fifteen campuses for the years 1994 through 2003 are employed to estimate the probability of remaining employed full time, entering phased retirement, or retiring fully (see Allen, Clark, and Ghent, 2004).

The tendency to enter phased retirement increases with age, as shown in Table 4.3. Less than 1 percent of eligible faculty aged fifty to fifty-four entered phased retirement in any year. The phased retirement rate for faculty between the ages of fifty-five and fifty-nine was 2.4 percent in 1997–2002 and 1.4 percent in 2002–2003. Between 3 and 5 percent of faculty aged sixty to sixty-four entered phased retirement, whereas 6 percent or more of faculty aged sixty-five and over became phased retirees.

The value of phased retirement is influenced by the type of pension plan in which the faculty member participates. Since 1971, UNC faculty have had the option of being included in the state employees' defined benefit plan or choosing to participate in an optional defined contribution plan. The state plan is a traditional defined benefit plan that determines benefits as 1.82 percent of final average earnings multiplied by years of service. Average earnings are based on the employee's highest four consecutive years of earnings. The plan has a five-year vesting requirement. The normal retirement age is sixty-five with five years of service; however, the plan also provides unreduced

Table 4.3. Retirement Rates for University of North Carolina System Faculty, by Year and Age Group

Age Group	1994–1996 Full	1997–2002 Full	1997–2002 Phased	2002–2003 Full	2002–2003 Phased
50–54	1.8	2.3	0.5	1.9	0.2
55–59	5.1	3.9	2.4	1.7	1.4
60–64	13.3	11.4	4.5	5.4	3.3
65	21.1	14.1	6.3	11.6	4.3
66–69	27.3	16.6	6.4	8.2	8.2
70+	26.3	14.3	7.4	9.1	9.1

Source: Annual census of faculty employment, UNC system.

retirement benefits with thirty years of service regardless of age or at age sixty with twenty-five years of service. Early retirement with reduced benefits is available at age fifty with twenty years of service or age sixty with five years of service (not coincidently, these are the eligibility conditions for the phased retirement plan). The optional retirement plans are defined contribution plans in which the employee contributes 6 percent of salary and the employer contributes 6.84 percent of salary.

Among faculty meeting the eligibility conditions for phased retirement during these years, approximately half are in the state plan and half are in a defined contribution plan. The UNC phased retirement plan requires faculty to retire prior to entering phased retirement. Thus, the pension benefit from the state plan is determined prior to starting phased retirement. This feature means that faculty in the defined benefit plan can combine a full retirement benefit with their half-time salary from phased retirement. As a result, many professors with service in excess of thirty years can have total income (earnings plus pension benefits) in phased retirement that is greater than their earnings from full-time employment. For example, a faculty member aged sixty with thirty years of service could retire and receive a pension benefit of 55 percent of their final average salary (1.82 times thirty years of service). Thus, while in phased retirement, the professor would be receiving a combined pension plus earnings from phased retirement of more than 100 percent of his or her final earnings. Faculty in the state retirement plan whose retirement benefits are growing rapidly with continued employment are less likely to enter phased retirement and are more likely to remain on the job full time.

Table 4.4 presents retirement rates for each year of the program for faculty in the state retirement plan and those in an optional retirement plan. The table reports both full and phased retirement rates by plan type. In each year, full retirement rates and phased retirement rates are greater for faculty in the state retirement plan than for those in the optional defined contribution

NEW DIRECTIONS FOR HIGHER EDUCATION • DOI 10.1002/he

Table 4.4. Retirement Rates for University of North Carolina System Faculty, by Year and Pension Plan

	State Pension Plan	ORP
1997–1998		
Full retirement	7.7	5.2
Phased retirement	4.4	1.6
1998–1999		
Full retirement	10.1	5.5
Phased retirement	3.1	1.4
1999–2000		
Full retirement	7.6	5.9
Phased retirement	5.5	2.0
2000–2001		
Full retirement	7.2	5.1
Phased retirement	4.4	2.5
2001–2002		
Full retirement	7.8	6.8
Phased retirement	3.6	1.1
2002–2003		
Full retirement	5.4	2.8
Phased retirement	4.5	1.2

Source: Annual census of faculty employment, UNC system.

plans. The phased retirement rate for those in the state plan is more than twice as large as for those in the defined contribution plans. This result is confirmed in our statistical analysis, where the predicted probability of entering phased retirement is 3.8 percent among those in the state plan and 1.6 percent for those in one of the optional retirement plans (Allen, Clark, and Ghent, 2004).

From a management perspective, universities would prefer that highly productive faculty remain on the job full time, while less productive faculty retire completely or enter phased retirement. To estimate what types of faculty select phased retirement, we examine retirement patterns as a function of the rate of growth of annual earnings. In the period we examined (1997–2000), faculty pay increases were entirely based on merit, as judged by deans and department heads. In the absence of a quantitative performance measurement system, pay raises are the best available indicator of performance. One would expect that highly productive faculty would receive larger annual salary increases than less productive faculty, and this continued growth in salary would encourage these faculty to remain on the job and not retire or enter phased retirement.

This prediction is borne out by the data. Compared to faculty who were receiving no real increases in salary, faculty with annual wage increases of 8 percent were 40 percent less likely to retire fully (5.9 percent compared to

10.3 percent annual retirement rates) and 60 percent less likely to enter phased retirement (1.7 percent compared to 4.3 percent annual probability of entering phased retirement). The same comparison can be made for faculty before the introduction of phased retirement in 1995–1997, when the odds of full retirement for faculty with 8 percent raises was 6.0 percent, well below the 12.0 percent odds for faculty with no raise. The total odds of retirement (full and phased combined) increased by 2.6 percent for faculty with no raises, compared to a 1.6 percent increase for faculty with 8 percent raises. Thus, the introduction of phased retirement had a differential impact on retirement rates between highly productive and less productive faculty, and this impact has the effect of modestly improving the productivity mix of faculty.

Retirement rates also differ by type of institution. Allen, Clark, and Ghent (2004) found that full retirement rates and phased retirement rates are much lower at UNC's Research I institutions (UNC at Chapel Hill and North Carolina State University) than at the Doctoral, Master's, and Baccalaureate campuses. At the Research I institutions, 1.6 percent of the eligible faculty entered phased retirement each year, while 3 to 4 percent of eligible faculty at the other types of institutions selected partial retirement. In comparison, the full retirement rates were 6.7 percent at the Research I institutions and between 8 and 12 percent per year at the other campuses.

On several occasions, UNC has surveyed faculty who selected phased retirement. Respondents were asked why they chose phased retirement over full retirement or full-time work. In two different surveys (1998 and 2003), over 60 percent of the faculty who entered the program indicated that they wanted to "gradually transition into retirement." Very few indicated that the reason they entered phased retirement was that they planned to "pursue other interests" (18 percent in 1998 and 9 percent in 2003). Other faculty cited poor health, changing university policies (including posttenure review), and an inability to afford full retirement as the dominant reasons for their entry into the phased retirement program.

The faculty surveys also explored changes in time allocation with phased retirement. Table 4.5 summarizes the shift in on-campus workloads after entering phased retirement. The average number of courses taught per year declined by about 50 percent (from 4.3 to 2.4). Interestingly, many of the faculty who entered phased retirement were academic administrators (32 percent of all phased retirees) who left administration, returned to a regular faculty position, and then entered phased retirement. Thus, the change in activities for these phased retirees often resulted in more teaching than when they were in administration. The surveys indicate that faculty allocated about the same percentage of their time to service and extension activities in phased retirement as they had done while working full time. The transition to phased retirement was associated with a slight increase in the proportion of time devoted to research; however, the total time spent conducting research declined.

Table 4.5. Faculty Workload on Campus, Before and After Entering Phased Retirement

	Before Phased Retirement	After Phased Retirement
Mean number of courses taught	4.3	2.4
	(2.8)	(1.7)
Mean percentage of time allocated to other activities:		
Research	27.6	29.6
	(26.8)	(36.2)
Public Service/Extension	7.4	7.3
	(12.7)	(18.4)
Administration/Institutional Service	24.2	9.9
	(30.0)	(18.8)
Other assignments	16.4	13.8
	(21.9)	(24.9)

Note: Standard deviations are reported in parentheses.

Source: Survey of UNC Phased Retirement Program Participants.

Survey responses indicated that the total annual income of phased retirees (including pensions and social security) was about 90 percent of their earnings before retirement. Given this relatively high level of income and reduced workloads, phased retirees at UNC expressed strong satisfaction with the phased retirement program. In the 2003 survey, 60 percent of phased retirees said that they strongly agreed with the statement, "I am pleased with my participation in the Phased Retirement Program and would make the same decision again." Another 33 percent agreed with this statement, and only 7 percent disagreed with the statement of support for their participation in phased retirement. In addition, almost 90 percent of phased retirees agreed with the statement that they "would recommend the Phased Retirement Program to my colleagues."

In summary, the phased retirement program at UNC is viewed as a valuable new employee benefit. Faculty who have entered the program seem highly satisfied with the phased retirement plan and are happy with the choice that they made to enroll in the plan. Another survey (Berberet and others, 2005) of active faculty age fifty and over indicates that over one-third of them are now planning to choose phased retirement instead of moving from full-time work to complete retirement. The introduction of the phased retirement program has been basically cost neutral, and there seem to have been relatively few administrative problems associated with phased retirement.

Conclusions and Implications

Universities face an unprecedented challenge of maintaining a high-quality faculty in an era of stagnant budgets, pressure for enrollment growth to accommodate the echo of the baby boom, and an all-time-high percentage of faculty in the fifty and over age bracket. Our research has shown that the introduction of phased retirement gives universities two crucial degrees of freedom in meeting this challenge. First, the separation rate of faculty increases significantly, especially for faculty between the ages of sixty and sixty-four. At a time when many campus leaders are worried that the end of mandatory retirement for faculty will result in a decline in retirement rates, this is an important offsetting force. Second, any fears that the introduction of phased retirement would hasten the departure of the most productive faculty to half-time jobs at other campuses or research institutes are completely unfounded. Instead, faculty who have become jaded with academic life are the ones who are most likely to embrace the phased retirement option.

UNC also benefits from the ability to improve personnel planning. Allen (2005) found that 59 percent of the surveyed deans and department heads thought that the introduction of phased retirement provided them with "an additional management tool for planning." In particular, it provided units with more time to develop a recruitment strategy, and the savings in salary budget gave the unit more freedom to meet staffing needs.

On the cost side, the main question is whether total labor cost—salary, benefits, and overhead—drops by 50 percent along with work effort. Employee benefits and overhead do decrease, and perhaps by even more than 50 percent for many types of faculty. Eligible faculty are eligible for the same health benefits regardless of their employment status (full-time work, phased retirement, or full retirement). The state actually saves money for those who enter phased retirement and become eligible for Medicare, which becomes the primary provider of medical insurance. UNC also saves the expense of contributing to the professor's pension plan. Certain overhead expenses, such as office and lab space and computers, do not diminish when a faculty member enters phased retirement. In disciplines where these overhead costs are significant, UNC is less likely to see a 50 percent cut in overall labor costs. A secondary concern is the cost of administering the policy, which requires a modest increase in the number of human resource professionals on campus.

Our research also shows that the introduction of phased retirement has had overwhelmingly favorable effects for UNC faculty. Most faculty who entered phased retirement were able to maintain 90 percent or more of their income while cutting their work obligations in half. Faculty also receive the less tangible benefit of being able to make a gradual transition to the next stage of their personal lives, adjusting to a retirement lifestyle while maintaining their identity as a faculty member.

NEW DIRECTIONS FOR HIGHER EDUCATION • DOI 10.1002/he

References

Allen, S. "The Value of Phased Retirement." In R. Clark and J. Ma (Eds.), *Recruitment, Retention, and Retirement in Higher Education: Building and Managing the Faculty of the Future.* Northampton, Mass.: Edward Elgar Publishing, 2005.

Allen, S., Clark, R., and Ghent, L. "Phasing into Retirement." *Industrial and Labor Relations Review,* 2004, 58(1), 112–127.

Berberet, J., and others. "Planning for the Generational Turnover of the Faculty: Faculty Perceptions and Institutional Practices." In R. Clark and J. Ma (Eds.), *Recruitment, Retention, and Retirement in Higher Education: Building and Managing the Faculty of the Future.* Northampton, Mass.: Edward Elgar Publishing, 2005.

Clark, R. "Changing Faculty Demographics and the Need for New Policies." In R. Clark and J. Ma (Eds.), *Recruitment, Retention, and Retirement in Higher Education: Building and Managing the Faculty of the Future.* Northampton, Mass.: Edward Elgar Publishing, 2005.

Clark, R., and d'Ambrosio, M. "Ignorance Is Not Bliss." *Research Dialogue* 78. New York: TIAA-CREF Institute, Dec. 2003.

Clark, R., and Ma, J. (Eds.). *Recruitment, Retention, and Retirement in Higher Education: Building and Managing the Faculty of the Future.* Northampton, Mass.: Edward Elgar Publishing, 2005.

Clark, R., and Rappaport, A. "The Changing Retirement Landscape." *Pension Section News,* Sept. 2001, pp. 14–19.

Ehrenberg, R. "Survey of Changes in Faculty Retirement Plans." 2003. http://www.aaup.org/Issues/retirement/retirepg.htm.

Ghent, L., Allen, S., and Clark, R. "The Impact of a New Phased Retirement Option on Faculty Retirement Decisions." *Research on Aging,* 2001, 23(6), 671–693.

Leslie, D., and Janson, N. "To Phase or Not to Phase: The Dynamics of Choosing Phased Retirement in Academe." In R. Clark and J. Ma (Eds.), *Recruitment, Retention, and Retirement in Higher Education: Building and Managing the Faculty of the Future.* Northampton, Mass.: Edward Elgar Publishing, 2005.

Switkes, E. "Phasing Out of Full Time Work at the University of California." In R. Clark and J. Ma (Eds.), *Recruitment, Retention, and Retirement in Higher Education: Building and Managing the Faculty of the Future.* Northampton, Mass.: Edward Elgar Publishing, 2005.

Watson Wyatt. *Phased Retirement: Reshaping the End of Work.* Washington, D.C.: Watson Wyatt, 1999.

STEVEN G. ALLEN *is associate dean for graduate programs and research in the College of Management, professor of business management and economics, and academic director of the M.B.A. program at North Carolina State University.*

ROBERT L. CLARK *is professor in the departments of economics and business management at North Carolina State University.*

LINDA S. GHENT *is associate professor of economics at Eastern Illinois University.*

5

Individuals who retire have widely varying needs and differ also in their preparedness for their new conditions.

The Costs and Benefits of Phased Retirement

David W. Leslie

On the whole, we found that phased retirement policies have served individuals and institutions well. But both individuals and institutions find themselves balancing advantages and disadvantages too. In this chapter, we assess who gains and who loses, and under what conditions. As with many such analyses, we conclude that it all depends on a variety of circumstances.

Phased retirement programs come in differing forms. They may be tightly restricted, so only a few faculty with years of seniority are eligible. Or they may be broadly available to anyone within a few years of normal retirement age. Faculty themselves vary in their readiness for and interest in retirement. Some prefer to leave well before they turn sixty-five, while others find it difficult to retire at all until they advance into their seventies. With so much variation among policies and individuals, we have found it difficult to generalize. But some cases have brought important issues to our attention. Our interviews provided us with candid insights into individuals and their concerns.

Individual Needs

Individuals approach retirement with a wide array of concerns. The most fundamental of these issues are health, finances, and family. Faculty in their late fifties or early sixties vary on these dimensions. Some of those we interviewed had already experienced age-related health issues and had struggled to recuperate from major heart or cancer surgery. Others had simply experienced

NEW DIRECTIONS FOR HIGHER EDUCATION, no. 132, Winter 2005 © Wiley Periodicals, Inc.
Published online in Wiley InterScience (www.interscience.wiley.com) • DOI: 10.1002/he.197

the onset of typical age-related declines in energy, acuity, and ability to manage complexity and change. One man nearing seventy reported being "mathematically worn out," but feeling dependent on the social support he received from associating with his faculty colleagues and enjoying campus activities. Another, at the pinnacle of a very successful career, felt he "couldn't continue to do it all."

We also found widely varying financial readiness for retirement. Some faculty had accumulated wealth, not only through prudent participation in retirement plans but through their own professional skills. Some had developed successful private practices or consulting relationships; others had written books that resulted in steady streams of royalties. Some highly successful entrepreneurs needed the time to develop these sources of income and, approaching retirement age, saw phasing as a way to make the transition to what amounted to a new (and sometimes lucrative) career.

Family circumstances often play a substantial role in the choices faculty make about retirement. Although one assumes that an individual in his or her sixties will have grown children and grandchildren, we found that more than a few had children in high school or college, requiring a steady income to meet the heavy demands of college tuition and related expenses. Some faculty we interviewed were working out marital issues. One had married for the second time and, having entered his seventies, was eager to spend time with a new spouse but felt committed to certain initiatives he had taken on the job. Others were working out the unfamiliar dynamic of relating to a spouse's retirement. Many acknowledged that new marital tensions emerged as retirement in any form meant spending more time with one's spouse than they had been accustomed to. As one person said, "[My spouse and I] mutually coined the phrase 'phased adjustment' to describe all the changes one must adapt to when leaving full-time work. The family side of it is as important as the work side." In all of these cases, the opportunity to step down from full-time work and devote more time to dealing with personal issues made impending retirement seem more feasible.

Psychologically, faculty seem often to identify intensely with their work. They are not just "professors." They are "chemists" or "mathematicians" or "economists." Retirement suggests that they will no longer be able to rely on the professional identity they have cultivated for thirty or forty years. "What do I become once I stop teaching and doing research?" asked one. "Do I stop being a historian?" The prospective psychological devastation this presents to some faculty prevents them from considering retirement, notwithstanding its inevitability. We were often told that going directly from full engagement in a professional career to full retirement was considered both painful and unhealthy.

One individual who had retired fully rather than phasing reported that he has regrets retiring so abruptly. As he finishes his last graduate students, he senses he is "losing the family": "Phased retirees would get the satisfaction of continuing their teaching and affiliation with students and colleagues." He felt that phasing was a healthy way to avoid the trauma of sudden, "cold turkey" retirement. Another mentioned "the value of continued relationships and professional contacts during the process of withdrawing from full-time work into retirement." In other words, the social props that have sustained an individual's identity through professional status can be at least temporarily maintained by phasing. Others agreed that phasing is a healthy way to navigate the trauma: "Retirement is hard to accept for academics. This is a way to dilute the shock of a cold turkey departure from a lifetime of work. I've been productive and active in a long career and was suddenly staring retirement in the face. It was not a pleasant prospect, so the phased option made it easier to do it gradually." The more gradual disengagement in phasing helps wean the immersed professional from total engagement and provides the opportunity to develop other interests and involvements.

Benefits to Individuals

The benefits to individuals of phased retirement are largely intangible. Phasing makes life easier, less stressful, and more tolerable, and it provides flexibility to handle a complicated major life transition.

Although phasing can mean less current income, time and money are fungible to some extent, especially for those at or near retirement age. For many who phase, the opportunity to control one's (remaining) time seems to increase substantially in value. Phasing usually means working half time. Most institutions among those we studied allow faculty to choose between working full time one semester and taking the second semester off, or working half time in both semesters. Both of these options meet individuals' needs, but the choice requires balancing personal needs with the demands of one's work.

Faculty whose work requires year-round involvement are more likely to elect to work half time both semesters. One example among those we interviewed was a music professor who worked with a choral group. He noted that this work required continuous involvement rather than a start-stop relationship with the students. Others reported that supervising graduate students' research also required continuous year-round involvement. Similarly, faculty with research grants could not easily abandon their work for a semester at a time.

At institutions with traditionally heavy teaching loads of up to four courses per semester, half-time work still amounts to a substantial effort. Teaching the full load for a single semester allows one to take the ensuing eight months off, an arrangement that some found to be a great relief.

Some faculty in their sixties were willing to acknowledge a declining ability to handle all aspects of their jobs with the same energy and effectiveness to which they had been accustomed. They professed relief at being able to shed responsibilities like committee service or administrative work that often came in addition to their primary interests in teaching or research. They also tended to realize that their own stake in decisions and policies was diminishing in proportion to their remaining time on the job: "I would personally prefer not to [serve on the promotion and tenure committee]. Some feel marginalized about being excluded, but I'd rather not be involved. Tenure decisions are about the future of the institution, and I'm on my way out. I don't have the same stake in it as younger faculty do, so they should be the ones to make the important decisions. I am also glad I don't have to attend any more faculty senate meetings!"

Whatever the rationale, phasing faculty valued the newly free time and put it to a variety of uses. Several reported buying property in warmer climates like Florida, the Carolinas, Arizona, or Hawaii and spending the winter months there. Some reported spending more time on recreational activities and hobbies. Those with grandchildren relished more frequent contact with them.

For some of the most professionally accomplished and engaged, phased retirement provided flexible time to begin new careers, to consult (internationally in some cases), or to tie up research projects for which they had funding. One person told us that he felt obliged to continue working to return value on the investment a federal agency had made in his work over many years. He might have preferred to fully retire, but phasing provided him with the opportunity to bring more of his research to closure. Others noted that they were committed to seeing their remaining doctoral students through their dissertation research.

As Allen, Clark, and Ghent note in Chapter Four, phased retirement may be more or less attractive in financial terms. Depending on terms of the policies under which they phase, individuals may experience a reduction in income during the phase period, or they may actually increase their income while phasing. In the more generous institutions, phasing meant a financial windfall. Participants in California State University's Faculty Early Retirement Program were eligible (as of 2004) to receive their full defined benefit pension and fully paid health insurance, and entitled to reemployment at 50 percent of their full-time salary for up to five years after formally retiring. Including social security, faculty in this system often made substantially more as half-time faculty than they did when working full time.

A small private liberal arts college provided an even more generous arrangement. Phased retirees agreed to teach half time for 70 percent of their full-time salary. Those who were eligible could also receive their full retirement annuities. The program was relatively popular: "The college was quite generous in its offer to pay me a lot of money to work half-time." It was particularly lucrative for at least one respondent to our survey: "My total income during the half-time period was slightly more than twice what

I would have received during my last year of teaching if I retired at age sixty-five and a half." Respondents at another small private college said their institution's plan resulted in more total compensation than they earned during their last year as full-time, tenured faculty.

In some cases, the university's support for health benefits was seen as another form of incentive: "I also like the security of the [university's] health insurance. My most serious concern is incurring bad health." A survey respondent said that "continuation of full medical benefits during phasing" was the principal reason for having elected to do so.

In cases where individuals are financially secure, they may find phasing attractive as a way to maintain a full income while cutting down on the time they spend working. One realized at age seventy that he could get full social security, he had to take distributions from his independent retirement accounts, and by working half time he would net the same income as he would from teaching full time. So there was a compelling logic for him to cut down to half-time work for what was, in effect, equal pay. "It was," he said, "pretty much an economic decision." Another said he "didn't need the university's money, so that wasn't an issue." He said the phased retirement program was structured generously enough to seriously consider retiring.

Our site visits and interviews took place in 2003 and 2004, when the retirement plans of many faculty had been affected by recent fluctuations in the stock market. A major decline will almost inevitably cause those in defined contribution plans who place assets in equities to delay retirement. The terms and conditions of their institutions' phased retirement policies allowed some to offset potential losses in the short run while putting off full retirement for several years.

If one's retirement income is at least ensured and other fundamental needs are met, then taking a pay cut to gain free time can be a very attractive option. A number of our respondents correspondingly cited their reduced and more flexible teaching schedule as a clear benefit. Some also noted that they were relieved to give up administrative and committee service obligations. As one respondent indicated, "[The terms of phased retirement are] reasonably attractive enough where buying the time for yourself is more important than the pay." An administrator responding to our survey confirmed that phased retirees do appreciate the opportunity to trade away pay for greater control over their time: "They give up 40 percent of their salary, but their teaching schedule is reduced and flexible."

Furthermore, institutions often typically provide full health and other benefits to phased retirees and often continue contributions to retirement funds. (Outlays by universities supporting phased retirement are therefore often far more than 50 percent of their outlays for faculty who have merely reduced their work assignment to half time and for whom universities had prorated payment for benefit premiums.)

Finally, although it might not be considered a benefit in the usual sense, we learned that some faculty elected to phase as a way to avoid post-tenure review.

Costs to Individuals

Phased retirement plans are not always financially attractive. The mix of incentives and benefits differentiates both the terms of the plans and the experience of those electing to phase. Although most plans are viewed favorably by those who provided us with their thoughts, they are not without some substantial penalties and disincentives either.

The most obvious disincentive is reduced pay. For faculty who are not yet eligible for social security or Medicare and who also elect the option before they can receive annuities from their provider, the reduction can be substantial and constraining. "The loss of income," as one put it and others agreed in varying terms, is perceived by many as the most unattractive aspect of phasing, even by those in the more generous programs.

Hidden costs emerged for some who phased. For example, one noted that deductions for insurance, parking, and other fees continued at the same rate for phased retirees as for full-time faculty. Others found themselves ineligible for merit raises, travel funds, grants, or summer or other supplemental employment. In some cases, policies had left these issues unaddressed; in others, misunderstandings had left phased retirees in a weaker position financially than they had anticipated. Although most plans are viewed very favorably by the faculty we interviewed, these policies are not without some substantial penalties and disincentives for individuals.

The most obvious disincentive is reduced gross income. For faculty who are not yet eligible for social security or Medicare and who may also elect the option before they can receive annuities from their provider, the reduction can be substantial and constraining. "The loss of income," as one put it, and as others agreed in varying terms, is perceived by many as the most unattractive aspect of phasing.

Public university faculty may participate in either private pension plans like TIAA-CREF or in state plans. The terms and conditions of these plans may differ substantially, making a phased retirement policy attractive to one group but unattractive to others. As one administrator pointed out, "I don't understand why anyone on our state retirement system would choose this [phased retirement] option because state retirement [a defined benefit plan] is based on the three most recent paid years and this reduces the last three years of pay [on which an individual's pension would be based]. It is more suitable for TIAA/CREF participants [a defined contribution plan]." A defined contribution plan provides that individuals set aside some of their income for retirement, usually supplemented by contributions from their institutions. The payout depends on how these funds have been invested and on performance by those investments. A defined benefit plan is common among public institutions. Retirees are guaranteed a given level of income, often based on an average of their last few years' salary, by an agency that may be funded by a state. If a defined benefit participant chooses to cut back to, say, 50 percent employment at 50 percent pay for several years prior to retirement, his or her retirement pay would be pegged to that level rather than to the salary the individual earned before phasing, a potentially devastating reduction.

Phased faculty are not always allowed to hold their office or lab space on the same terms as when they worked full time. In some cases, they have to share office space or do without, and those with labs and substantial grants may have to bring both to an end—an orderly end, if possible. The institutions we visited or surveyed had largely dealt with these issues by negotiating with individual retirees, but the problems were clearly a source of tension in a few cases. Most institutions felt severe space pressures, especially for labs. They needed all the space they could get for newer faculty and were anxious to provide as much incentive as they could to those just getting their research programs started. The consequences of pitting younger faculty against older faculty included some—usually subterranean—generational tension. The upshot for individuals was a feeling that they were being pressured to give up their space and access to support services.

Faculty are anxious about the common element of phased retirement policies requiring them to waive their tenure rights and terminate their employment on a certain date in the future. One reported appreciating the opportunity to retire by gradually phasing down, but noted that to be eligible for the university's generous severance payment to all fully retiring faculty, it was necessary "to terminate my employment at age sixty-eight whether I feel ready to or not." Another said, "The only drawback to the program that I've detected so far is the four-year time limit for participation. Perhaps I will be ready to retire fully. . . . But I may not be, in which case the limitation would be irksome."

Phasing faculty have different experiences in how their departments treat them. They have almost always been well-regarded senior faculty, enjoying the respect and deference of their colleagues and students. But phasing involves ratcheting down one's commitments and involvements, as well as one's physical presence, in the day-to-day life of the department and campus. In many cases, phasing involves an extended absence. If one arranges a full-time assignment for, say, the fall semester alone, it may mean a full eight months (say, spring semester plus summer) away. It becomes progressively more difficult to stay in touch as new faculty come to the department and as one loses track of the day-to-day life of the institution. One person noted, "I feel a little disconnected from the department. I miss things that happened while I was away and don't know what people are talking about at meetings. . . . Decisions flow continuously, and I can't always play a part. Some of these decisions now affect me less, but others do, and I don't feel I have a commensurate say."

Our interviews were spiced with descriptions of the subjective experience of phasing, like being "disconnected" or "marginalized," feeling "ignored" or "irrelevant," losing "clout" or "influence." Struggling to describe this sense of gradual disengagement, one of our interviewees said, "The ambiguity of one's status [in phased retirement] doesn't clearly define one as retired or not. Colleagues may view a person as retired, although he continues to make a contribution. He feels more of a disconnect with the department. People don't seek you out; you feel more marginalized. When you give up tenure, as phased retirees do, you give up service assignments, committee work, etc. So you are less well connected. You may also not teach some important courses you once taught."

Phasing faculty may also diminish their involvement in national organizations. Several suggested that they had stopped attending professional meetings and were losing touch with developments in their disciplines.

The generational gap between phasing faculty and newer, more cutting-edge faculty taking their positions was also substantial. This gap was both intellectual and social. Faculty with newer degrees may have very different ideas about substance and about teaching. We heard one eloquent phased retiree discuss his disapproval of younger faculty's approach to the field, indicating that phasing gave him the opportunity to distance himself from a changing department.

Socially and professionally, the lives of older and younger faculty are different. Younger faculty tend to live farther away from campus and tend to have children in school. They are, we were told, less involved in campus life and informal relations at the department level. They also face a different standard for tenure and promotion than older faculty did a generation ago. As our interviews suggested, research has become far more central to the process, and teaching and university service less central. So junior faculty are more likely to focus on their own individual agendas than on the common good of the department and its students. These different realities and the related tensions may lead older faculty who are not quite ready to retire fully to find phasing attractive. But they also contribute to increasing frustration for those who phase, as they see change all around them while their own influence and involvement diminish.

Another issue that affects older faculty is the generational change in students. A long-time administrator pointed out "an age gap between students and the older faculty," and he recognized that it makes relating to these students and teaching them harder as the gap widens. We were told elsewhere that younger students tend to be "purely visual," that they "don't read, and can't or won't write." Frustration with students may lead faculty to elect phased retirement, but it also weighs heavily on those who do phase, making their work harder and less rewarding with each passing year.

NEW DIRECTIONS FOR HIGHER EDUCATION • DOI 10.1002/he

Costs and Benefits for Institutions

Overall, institutions see phased retirement as a benign and humane policy that helps faculty retire in more orderly and predictable ways than might be the case after uncapping of the mandatory retirement age. However, in cases where formalized phased retirement policies are either too restrictive or too generous, enticing too few or encouraging too many to commit to its terms, the institution may experience unintended and debilitating consequences.

Departments see a double-edged effect of phased retirement in terms of their relationship with senior faculty. The costs of offering phased retirement, both financial and programmatic, can be much greater than intended. Scarce resources are locked in, and program flexibility is sometimes constrained by long-term commitments to phased retirees. But retaining experienced senior faculty also provides continuity in programs that might otherwise be affected by too many retirements, and phased retirees may provide broader and more skilled coverage in departments that face staffing difficulties. As one administrator said, "The institution wins. . . . Phasees actually work more than half time. They tend to continue with their research on top of the assigned teaching, so they are really working more like three-quarters time for half pay. [Professor X], for example, is a very popular teacher, and teaches large classes, in addition to remaining a prominent [scholar in his discipline]."

The value of retaining senior faculty who have been loyal campus citizens for many years provides an intangible, but very real benefit to one institution: "The [phased retirees] tend to have been the workhorses of [this campus]. They have mostly been here for thirty years or so, and they are accustomed to pitching in and doing what they are asked. This is much different from the newer faculty, who expect to negotiate reduced loads right from the start." Another administrator reported, "On balance, the institution benefits. It retains senior, experienced faculty with institutional memory. They can serve as mentors to grad students and junior faculty. They help departments maintain perspective on administrative issues."

Phased retirement presents both the individual and the institution an opportunity to negotiate a new and different work assignment. We interviewed one who had spent his career as a "rats-in-mazes" psychologist with a long record of external funding. When he decided to phase, he agreed to give up his lab and take on a heavy teaching load. At the time of our interview, he was teaching a thirteen-hundred-student introductory course and found it very rewarding. The payoff to the department was obvious: the productivity of this arrangement meant junior faculty were freer to pursue their research in lieu of teaching.

This may have been an anomalous case, as we also interviewed faculty who had elected to phase because they felt overburdened or ineffective in their teaching. In a few cases, academic disciplines had declined in funding and popularity, leaving too many senior faculty dealing with too few students. Phasing was a way to find different assignments for them and to reduce the institution's costs as well.

But phased retirement can also encourage valued people to downshift their work at the peak of their careers. Departments lose more than just half of a teaching resource; phased retirees often withdraw from (or are ineligible for) committee service, advising, research, and mentoring. One administrator noted, "Unfortunately, some of the best people take the phased option." Since individuals covered by a policy have the right to phase or not, deans or chairs have little influence over who may elect this option.

We think that one of the most compelling of our findings from a policy standpoint may be that faculty generally state that they plan to retire voluntarily at a fairly traditional age—between sixty-four and sixty-six. It follows, then, that a phased retirement policy could err in two fundamental ways. It might err by making it more attractive for faculty to continue working full time because their pay or their pensions on a phased appointment would not support them adequately. Or it could err by enticing those who would retire at the typical age to elect an alternative that costs the institution more. (Among men, the average base salary for those who would retire and work part time was higher by about four thousand dollars a year than for those who would not, suggesting that those best prepared economically for retirement would nevertheless be willing to continue working part time for reasons other than economic need.)

Phased retirement plans help to give institutions and departments early signals about who will retire, when, and how. These policies typically require participants to waive their tenure rights as of the date they commit to retiring fully. Absent a mandatory retirement age, phased retirement plans give institutions the ability to plan and manage their resources with more certainty than would otherwise be possible. Institutions also retain a substantial fraction of phased retirees' compensation that can be reallocated in line with strategic needs and priorities. Departments may feel they lose when phased positions are reallocated. Or they may feel more burdened when they have to manage more part-time faculty without promise of full-time replacements for their phased retirees. Department chairs, deans, and provosts have to add these issues to their plans—issues that can be contentious if not carefully managed.

Also, the marketplace for faculty has seen escalating competition (and compensation) for junior faculty, especially in states like California where enrollment pressures, lagging state appropriations, and housing costs make it difficult to find the people most institutions need so badly. Hiring junior faculty is complicated by competition from peer institutions that may be able to sweeten their offers with reduced teaching loads and more support during the initial pretenure years. Institutions with attractive phased retirement policies may find that they are losing senior faculty at a rate that forces them to resort to hiring adjunct or temporary faculty as the only way they can stretch scarce dollars to meet student demand. The California State University system has been particularly afflicted because the generous terms of its phased retirement policy now attract so many of its retirees, locking positions and money in place for up to five years while extraordinary enrollment pressure, coupled with static or decreased funding, is unrelenting (Council for Aid to Education, 1997).

On the whole, though, institutions find that phased retirement policies are helpful to individual faculty, improve morale, and are mainly disruptive to departments that lose too many senior people in a short time.

Reference

Council for Aid to Education. *Breaking the Social Contract: The Fiscal Crisis in Higher Education.* Santa Monica, Calif.: Rand, 1997. http://www.rand.org/publications/CAE/CAE100/.

DAVID W. LESLIE *is Chancellor Professor of Education at the College of William and Mary.*

6

Those who address questions about phased retirement policies should see them in a larger context of needs for flexibility in the terms of faculty employment.

Policy-Related Issues and Recommendations

David W. Leslie, Natasha Janson, Valerie Martin Conley

We focus in this chapter on a few basic questions underlying the rationale for and framing of phased retirement policies. Our overall conclusion is that in the absence of mandatory retirement, policies need to strike a balance between the needs and interests of individuals and institutions. Both face inexorable realities. Individuals age and change, and they will have to choose how they leave the active workforce. Options give them a sense of control and accommodate the varied ways in which they adapt to advancing years.

Institutions operate in a dynamic environment in which the body of knowledge grows and is reshaped constantly. Students bring new interests and ambitions to their studies. Competitive excellence demands a continued quest for the cutting edge in teaching, research, and service. Funding seems to get tighter in every passing year, requiring more strategic reallocation of positions and faculty effort than ever before.

These realities have led as many as half of all colleges and universities to acknowledge the need for varied retirement options. Early retirement, phased retirement, and retirement incentives of various kinds have been initiated as ways to promote turnover among faculty at or approaching traditional retirement age.

As we have looked in depth at how phased retirement works, we have found a more complex interaction between varied individual approaches to retirement and varied needs and strategies among their employing institutions.

NEW DIRECTIONS FOR HIGHER EDUCATION, no. 132, Winter 2005 © Wiley Periodicals, Inc.
Published online in Wiley InterScience (www.interscience.wiley.com) • DOI: 10.1002/he.198

We look at these complexities and outline some basic issues institutions need to think through as they consider phased retirement policies or implement the policies they now rely on.

How Do Faculty Retire?

Our analysis suggests that faculty normally retire between ages sixty-four and sixty-six, but that significant numbers prefer to retire earlier, later, or in stages. Men and women show differing tendencies in their retirement preferences and patterns. Income, job satisfaction, family, and workload variables play slightly different roles for the genders. With the very large majority of retirements likely to be men in the near-term future, it appears to us that flexible work arrangements will be increasingly appealing to men who pass age sixty before retiring. In the case of women, flexible employment options appear equally appealing over the course of their career and may prompt more decisions to phase into retirement prior to age sixty. If true, this presents a dilemma to a profession that has had difficulty attracting women and may increasingly lose them to earlier retirements.

Predicting the probability that any individual would retire at a given age or date is difficult. In fact, we find that uncertainty about a particular retirement age or date increases as individual faculty grow older. This is probably an unanticipated consequence of prohibiting mandatory retirement. At one time, individuals knew with greater certainty that they would have to retire at, say, age sixty-five. Now, with more freedom to choose and more options at many institutions, faculty appear less committed to any particular choice. That means it is far more likely today that faculty need the opportunity to find terms and conditions for retirement that accommodate their own individual circumstances.

We find that the better-paid and more successful academics, particularly men, are more likely to continue working until or beyond age seventy. But unmarried women whose pay appears not to have kept pace with men's pay also are more likely to elect to work past age sixty-five, perhaps because retirement seems less affordable or because they value the social support they enjoy on the job. We estimate this population to be on the order of 14 percent of all tenured faculty at four-year institutions (Leslie and Conley, 2003). Women constitute a much larger proportion of those who would consider retiring early than they do of the population of faculty in general. Family considerations almost certainly play a large part. Spousal income appears to correlate with women's interest in early or phased retirement, for example. Also, work issues, such as carrying a heavy teaching load, appear to affect the age at which women consider retiring.

Although sixty-five is a reasonably good estimate of the average retirement age for faculty, it is only an average. In the absence of any mandatory retirement age, greater and greater variability appears to have emerged in when and how faculty choose to leave active work. Institutions may need to know a lot more about this variability than they usually do. Understanding when and how faculty prefer to step away from full-time employment might help develop a wider array of options and possibilities. If colleges and universities provide enough options to accommodate the range of faculty interests, they may be able to manage retirement processes and patterns more precisely and more effectively.

We should point out that knowing more should include an assessment of retirement plans for younger faculty. As the proportion of women faculty grows and as the generational norms of work evolve, it appears to us that there will be increasing interest in flexible employment arrangements of all kinds, and particularly for a period of flexible work before retirement. Data from the National Study of Postsecondary Faculty survey show that younger faculty (those now under age fifty) plan to retire earlier than the current generation. In fact, both men and women plan to retire about three years earlier, a substantial and unexpected shift downward if it should be borne out in reality.

The Need for Flexible Employment

Institutions will undoubtedly want to shape their employment policies, including retirement policies, around the expectations of the coming generations, especially because signs point to an increasingly tight market for new faculty. With large numbers of (mostly) male retirees now entering prime retirement years and the need to attract their replacements, who will far more likely be female than ever before, the academic profession must be seen as a more accommodating arena for work and careers.

A number of recent reports confirm the disparity between increasing numbers of terminal degrees awarded to women and lagging indicators of career entry and success (Chronicle of Higher Education, 2004). Women are underrepresented in many academic disciplines but overrepresented in traditional fields such as education and nursing, and their rates of publication, research grant awards, and time-on-the-job measures all tend to lag behind those of men. Women are more likely to take part-time and non-tenure-track jobs in lower-status institutions than are men. They are also more likely to retire earlier than men.

Women make a greater sacrifice in choosing an academic career. Over three-quarters (77 percent) of men under age forty who have terminal degrees and positions at research or doctoral universities are married (or cohabiting), while only 62 percent of women are married (or cohabiting). Career-long, tenure-eligible full-time women faculty at research and doctoral universities are far less likely to be married than male faculty in the same age cohort. Among the younger women who have invested heavily in academic career success, 57 percent report having no dependents. Only 34

Figure 6.1. Total Hours Worked per Week: All Full-Time Faculty, by Number of Dependents and Gender

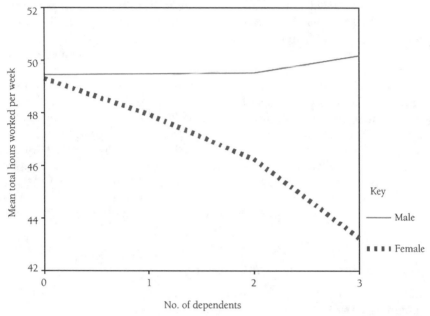

percent of men in the same situation report having no dependents. So women appear to have been much more likely to forgo marriage and children if they choose academic careers. In short, the route to a fully successful academic career seems to work against women's chances.

When women do marry and have children, the academic workplace handicaps them for these commitments. Having dependents disadvantages women while advantaging men. Figure 6.1 shows the effect of having dependents on the number of hours worked per week.

The effects of having children on women's research activity, and therefore on their ability to succeed over the long term, is marked. Figure 6.2 shows a steady, linear decline in the average number of hours women spend on research compared to a slight increase for men. The effect is clearly to women's competitive disadvantage. Mason and Goulden (2004) have reached a similar conclusion using data from the National Science Foundation's Survey of Doctoral Recipients.

Although further work is needed on this topic, our preliminary analysis shows that both hours on the job and hours on research correlate positively with a composite measure of career success. This composite measure includes an individual's salary, rank, type of institution, and tenure status. The conclusion, then, is that the academic workplace needs to be more

**Figure 6.2. Hours Worked per Week on Research: All Full-Time
Faculty, by Number of Dependents and Gender**

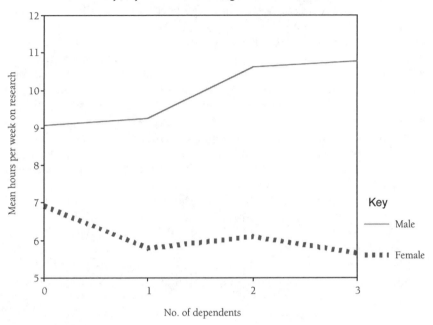

accommodating if younger women faculty with family responsibilities are
going to succeed. More important, young women who aspire to achieve in
academe need to see that institutions are committed to their success at work
and career.

That visible commitment will most clearly be demonstrated by policies
that allow more flexibility than earlier generations have enjoyed and provide more affirmative compensation for the disadvantages that marriage and
family pose (statistically speaking) for women.

Flexible Employment Policies Are a Good Investment

Flexible employment provides net value added. Typically one thinks of less
than full-time (or less than overtime) employment as being somehow of
less worth. But this represents stereotypical and short-term thinking
because it fails to account for the investment colleges and universities make
in the development of talent. Thinking in terms of career development,
flexible employment makes sense. Younger faculty's circumstances vary.
Equal treatment makes sense if everyone starts at the same point, but the
evidence establishes clearly that everyone does not. So if the goal is to
attract, hold, and develop the best and the brightest, we need to think in

NEW DIRECTIONS FOR HIGHER EDUCATION • DOI 10.1002/he

terms of policies that will maximize the return on an institution's invest-ment—policies that accommodate individual differences.

These differences include clear and important gender differences dur-ing prime childbearing years, as well as differences in circumstances that affect how people retire. Because recruiting current and future generations of faculty will depend on how attractive the workplace and career prospects are to women and to men who may increasingly play more substantial roles in family life than their fathers did, flexible employment options need to become the norm rather than grudgingly provided exceptions for individu-als. Prospective faculty need to see that institutions are prepared to affir-matively accommodate their marital and family circumstances, or they will look to employment outside academe, an alternative our increasingly pressed colleges and universities cannot afford in the face of the rapid aging of current faculty and a tougher economic reality.

In this conclusion, we agree with the 2005 report of the Office of Women in Higher Education at the American Council on Education, *An Agenda for Excellence: Creating Flexibility in Tenure-Track Faculty Careers.* Citing the need to compete for talent in a global marketplace, the "Agenda" explicitly recognizes the need to "evaluate and act on all aspects of faculty career cycles" (p. 3). The report focuses on how more flexibility at all stages of faculty careers serves individuals' and institutions' interests.

The Corporate Need for Flexibility

Just as we see a growing interest in and demonstrable need for flexible employment for individuals, so too is the dynamic and competitive mar-ketplace affecting universities' needs. Although it may have been possible at one point, say, in 1940, when the AAUP Statement on Academic Freedom and Tenure (American Association of University Professors, 2004) was adopted and the foundations for academic employment policy were virtu-ally chipped in stone, to visualize the academic marketplace as uniform across campuses and disciplines, the vast changes in higher education over the past sixty-five years beg for reform.

While these changes probably affect the entire life course and career tra-jectory of all faculty, they are particularly profound for younger and older faculty. More newly hired faculty are, and will continue to be, far more female than ever before. And with no mandatory retirement age, older fac-ulty are freer than ever before to choose the time, place, and manner of their retirement.

At the same time, colleges and universities are increasingly pressed by increasing demand (in most states) and tighter funding, as well as an increas-ingly global competition for reputation and faculty. Jones (2002–2003) noted, "The National Science Foundation concluded that overall labor market conditions have been good for new doctorate recipients over the past decade, with *gains most notable in nonacademic sectors*" (p. 33). Against this competition with nonacademic employers, higher education is constrained by tight funding and increasingly unattractive working conditions and career prospects. Jones's report asserts:

> Without the necessary funds, colleges and universities may be forced to find alternate ways of dealing with increasing enrollments, such as increasing class sizes or faculty workloads. Reliance on non-faculty, such as graduate assistants and postdoctoral students for teaching and research, might increase as well. Colleges and universities also may not replace retiring professors or may rely increasingly on part-time or non-tenure track faculty to teach classes. In fact, lower paid part-time or adjunct positions have been growing at a faster rate than full-time positions. And although employment of adjunct instructors is more prevalent among 2-year institutions, this trend is also a concern for 4-year institutions. Some faculty members may prefer part-time employment, but poor labor market conditions may impel others who want full-time positions to take adjunct positions that offer little potential for upward mobility [p. 32].

Baldwin and Chronister (2002) chronicled this substitution of non-tenure-eligible faculty in increasing numbers of faculty positions. For new Ph.D.s who have invested years in preparation, the prospect of relatively low-paying work without prospect of long-term security can only discourage interest in academic careers. Coupled with the pressures and constraints that make tenure-track positions more challenging for those with family responsibilities, institutions will have to develop more attractive work and career options for the best and brightest prospects.

Developing Phased Retirement and Other Flexible Employment Policies

The major premise, then, from which our policy recommendations flow is that a variety of pressures are converging that argue for flexible employment arrangements for faculty. If the profession is going to be seen as an attractive opportunity in both the way work is structured and rewarded and the way career options allow for family at one stage and individualized retirement planning at a later stage, the next generations of faculty will want to see more of a commitment to flexibility than has been the case with previous generations.

Our study concluded that a number of significant issues have surfaced as colleges and universities experiment with phased retirement plans for their faculty. For example, we have found:

• A persistent tension between establishment of clear and consistent policies about the terms and conditions for phased retirement and the need for individualization of those terms and conditions to meet the widely varied circumstances in which individual faculty make their decisions.

• Departments are affected differently, depending on the profile of their faculty. Some value their more experienced colleagues and the expertise and status they provide. Others simply lose half of a faculty position and find themselves temporizing with nontenure-track substitutions for a period of years.

• Phased retirement policies may be too broadly or too narrowly drawn. On one hand, they may encourage too many faculty to phase and at too great a cost both financially and academically. On the other hand, they may be so conservatively drawn that few faculty elect to phase, failing to serve as an incentive to encourage retirement.

• Institutions may lack a clear data-based analysis of their faculty workforce and its retirement plans. Framing a policy without knowing whom it might affect and how it might be perceived is essentially taking a shot in the dark.

• Deans and department chairs are critical to the implementation of any retirement policy. While they should not be put in the position of offering financial advice or other advice (for example, psychological counseling or marital counseling) they are not qualified to provide, they should have a clear and current understanding of the institution's policies and should be encouraged to feed back their experiences with individual faculty.

• Having a policy on the books provides deans and chairs an opening to discuss phased retirement with faculty who become eligible. Many of those we interviewed felt this helped advance individuals' planning for retirement whether they chose to phase or not.

• The costs to the institution of phased retirement plans should be weighed against the benefits. Actual dollar outlays may be relatively small once balanced against actual dollar savings in compensation. Institutions gain commitments from individuals to relinquish tenure rights and may also recapture office and lab space and other resources that accrue to a senior faculty position. They recoup a substantial fraction of a comparatively high salary and may well be retaining services of a highly valued individual who would otherwise leave the campus. Exposure of the institution is limited by terms and conditions of the policy, as well as by the number of faculty who are eligible and elect to phase.

• Phased retirement is only one way in which institutions may provide for flexible employment. Adopting a philosophical commitment to flexing for all faculty may be a competitive necessity as the market in which faculty are recruited changes. Flexing sends a strong signal about the value an institution places on support for its faculty.

NEW DIRECTIONS FOR HIGHER EDUCATION • DOI 10.1002/he

Conclusions and Recommendations

The demographics of faculty retirement do not appear to have changed as much after the end of mandatory retirement as most institutions assumed they would. In general, faculty do not plan to remain on the job much beyond the standard retirement age of sixty-five. Nor does it appear that faculty have responded in great numbers to incentive programs designed to encourage either early or phased retirement.

While data from National Study of Postsecondary Faculty show that as many as half of all faculty express an interest in phased retirement, only about 4 percent in the prime age groups have actually elected to phase. It appears to us that the potential variability of motives to retire and preferred patterns of retirement have not been fully accommodated in policies that were designed to provide attractive options.

We think many existing policies reflect an ambivalence of purpose: they provide incentives for faculty to retire in predictable and orderly fashion, but often seem designed conservatively to limit the numbers who might elect to phase. More generous programs do seem to encourage more participation. But financial incentives alone are a blunt instrument, helping neither individuals nor institutions to successfully navigate the complex process—a mix of financial, career, psychological, and social factors—that affects decisions to retire. Nor do "blunt instrument" plans help institutions navigate the strategic and workforce issues that emerge as faculty take up the options they are offered.

Obviously a deeper understanding of all of these factors is needed. We have found that retirement is a profoundly individual process, with decisions often being made at the intersection of many considerations that can be uncontrollable. On the whole, faculty, like others, will retire at a reasonably predictable age, although there may well be more variability among faculty than among the general population.

However, if both men and women perceive a supportive environment and have a hand in making informed choices about how to retire, they appear willing to renegotiate the terms and conditions of their employment. Thoughtful navigation of this complex and little-understood process can serve both individuals and institutions well, particularly if both sides have enough freedom (and wisdom) to bend to one another's interests. We think the research showing greater satisfaction with retirement choices in which individuals felt empowered to choose strongly supports negotiated rather than strictly standardized phased retirement agreements.

As desirable as individually negotiated agreements about retirement may be, there is great potential for discrimination unless these negotiations fall within a policy that clearly specifies eligibility to participate, outlines acceptable terms and conditions of employment, and establishes principles concerning pay and benefits. Otherwise individual arrangements could be much different from department to department or even individual to individual—and based on no more than a chair's or dean's whim.

Faculty appear to consider an increasingly complex and profoundly individual set of issues that affect their decisions about when to retire. Some faculty see ongoing rewards, psychic and material, in continuing to work. In a good proportion of cases, that means a different kind of work: teachers may turn to research or service and researchers to teaching, for example. Others want to pursue different pleasures: new career challenges, travel, hobbies, warmer climates, living closer to grandchildren, playing more golf, or caring for a family member. This suggests that more options and more flexibility in choosing among the options would serve both retirees and institutions better than the one-size-fits-all approach.

One implication may be that the older the individual is, the more flexible the phased retirement options should be. A policy might in fact allow an individual to trade flexibility of options against length of the term. Older potential phased retirees might opt for greater flexibility of choice in work assignment while accepting a shorter term of eligibility. Conversely, younger potential phased retirees might be more willing to accept given work assignments in exchange for a longer term.

Institutions can help the decision along by focusing on the basic security issues: adequate income, health insurance, access to professional colleagues, and support for their work. Beyond this, and attention to equity for all, retirement is so much an individual matter that the standardized terms of policies may have only minor effects. Deans and chairs are not particularly well prepared to counsel their senior faculty or negotiate retirement arrangements in a way that allows individuals to meet their needs. But careful attention to the process, respecting and regarding individual interests in a way that allows productive disengagement, may build goodwill among those who are considering retirement. Supporting them with personal, professional, and financial counsel might alleviate the need to provide expensive incentives like golden parachutes that are designed to attract people to retirement through one-time financial windfalls.

There is, at bottom, no way to guarantee that individuals eligible for phased retirement will elect it. We have heard often enough that "those who we'd hope wouldn't retire" have been among the most enthusiastic participants (and conversely, as well). Phased retirement may have persuaded some to retire sooner, but not as many as might have been expected. And as one administrator pointed out, the availability of a phased retirement option provides an opening to talk with individuals about their plans.

Key Conclusions. Our study affirms that goals of retirement policies should be explicit. Institutions may want to encourage retirements or encourage retention, depending on their strategic position. With that major premise in mind, we revisit some of the key findings of our study:

- Age is the main determinant of retirement. Institutions should have good data on the age profile of their faculty by discipline.
- Our interviews suggested that more faculty would elect phased or early retirement than currently do if policies were more accommodating and information about options were more clearly communicated.
- Responses to incentives will vary according to individuals' age, gender, wealth, health, workload, and satisfaction. But responses will be highly individual (and therefore random, in a statistical sense, as well).
- Mutuality is at least as important as standardizing terms and conditions in phased retirement policies.
- Flexibility in accommodating individual interests must be balanced against the need for fair and equitable treatment of all eligible retirees, as well as against the institution's goals and resources.
- Senior faculty who phase can add value in both conventional (credit-generating courses, grant-funded research) and unconventional (preserving institutional memory, mentoring, advising) work roles. Value-added rather than formula-based assignments should be part of the mutuality agreement.

Policy Recommendations. The following recommendations draw on results of the studies reported in this volume. We intend for them to help institutions frame the goals and provisions of policies supporting increasingly varied choices that faculty are making about when and how to retire.

- Faculty should be involved in developing policies, in part because recognizing their interests will promote more realistic policies and in part because their involvement will help broaden awareness of the institution's good faith and of the policies themselves.
- We recommend that institutions provide broad eligibility to phase and terms that will encourage individuals to phase as long as mutuality can be satisfied.
- Pay, benefits, and general guidelines on length of term, workload, and other conditions such as access to office or lab space and support services should be established at the institutional level. Specific details about actual work assignments should be negotiable, subject to review and approval for consistency, at the department level.
- Faculty approaching retirement may need comprehensive financial planning support, and some may need more personal counseling. While colleges and universities may not be in a position to provide it, they should routinely recommend financial planning as early as ten to fifteen years prior to the time when faculty will reach a predictable retirement age. They should also be prepared to assist in locating other resources faculty may need as they consider phasing.
- Individual circumstances may require special consideration and may be essential to securing an agreement. Institutions should be prepared to be flexible in exceptional cases.

- Faculty who elect to phase often feel marginalized and disenfranchised. Deans, chairs, and colleagues should understand the social and psychological vulnerabilities associated with partial or full retirement as individuals disengage from the professional and social activities on which their identities have depended for many years. Supportive gestures and continuing respect for phased retirees should be routine.
- Departments should be provided incentives to encourage phased retirements. To the extent possible, salaries and benefits vacated by phasing individuals should be returned to the most affected departments. If larger strategic considerations prevent such redistribution, the principles by which decisions are made should be clearly communicated. (Of course, once an individual fully retires, then the department will have to make its case anew for the position and the funding.)
- Departments that find themselves unduly affected by many simultaneous phased retirements ought not to be penalized either advertently or inadvertently. They may need rebuilding with an accelerated infusion of new positions and support beyond anyone's expectations. Although it may be tempting to put limits on what fraction of a department's faculty may phase at any given time or to impose a queuing requirement to spread phasing out, it is probably more important to provide departments with incentives to encourage phasing.
- Long-term planning should allow an increasing interest in flexible employment options. Women represent an increasing fraction of the academic workforce and show greater interest in flexibility at all career stages. Therefore, it is likely that the overall number of faculty who will consider phased retirement in the future seems likely to increase. As we have noted, the availability of flexing makes academic employment more attractive in a highly competitive marketplace.
- Phased retirement programs at individual institutions should be evaluated to assess the outcomes and compared with outcomes of programs with different provisions so new policies can build on others' successes. More public sharing of experiences among institutions would help to identify the most successful practices.

On the whole, we suggest that phasing into retirement could serve more individuals and more institutions better. If policies can be framed to promote win-win solutions to the needs of both sides, phasing will undoubtedly become a more legitimate and popular way to navigate the inevitable ends of many careers in the near and foreseeable future. But as one respondent said, "The devil is in the details. What is the retiree's right? What is negotiable? What is the institution's right? And who is responsible for what?" Exploration and experimentation with these issues and a greater understanding of the needs of faculty as they retire, as well as further monitoring of programs' successes and challenges, should be continued.

References

American Association of University Professors. *1940 Statement of Principles on Academic Freedom and Tenure with 1970 Interpretive Comments*. Washington, D.C.: American Association of University Professors, 2004. http://www.aaup.org/statements/Redbook/1940stat.htm.

American Council on Education. *An Agenda for Excellence: Creating Flexibility in Tenure-Track Faculty Careers*. Washington, D.C.: American Council on Education, 2005. http://www.acenet.edu/bookstore/pdf/2005_tenure_flex_summary.pdf.

Baldwin, R., and Chronister, J. *Teaching Without Tenure: Policies and Practices for a New Era*. Baltimore: Johns Hopkins University Press, 2002.

Chronicle of Higher Education. "Women in Higher Education: A Special Report." Dec. 3, 2004, p. 1. http://chronicle.com/weekly/v51/i15/15a01001.htm.

Jones, E. "Beyond Supply and Demand: Assessing the Ph.D. Job Market." *Occupational Outlook Quarterly*, Winter 2002–0303. http://www.bls.gov/opub/ooq/2002/winter/art03.pdf.

Leslie, D., and Conley, V. "Early and Phased Retirement Plans Among Tenured Faculty: A First Look." Paper presented at the Annual Meeting of the Association for the Study of Higher Education, Portland, Ore., Nov. 13, 2003.

Mason, M., and Goulden, M. "Do Babies Matter (Part II)? Closing the Baby Gap." *Academe,* 2004, *90*(6). Retrieved from http://www.aaup.org/publications/Academe/2004/04nd/04ndmaso.htm.

David W. Leslie is Chancellor Professor of Education at the College of William and Mary.

Natasha Janson is a graduate student and research assistant at the College of William and Mary.

Valerie Martin Conley is assistant professor of higher education and associate director of the Center for Higher Education at Ohio University.

NEW DIRECTIONS FOR HIGHER EDUCATION • DOI 10.1002/he

INDEX

Back Issue/Subscription Order Form

Copy or detach and send to:
Jossey-Bass, A Wiley Imprint, 989 Market Street, San Francisco CA 94103-1741

Call or fax toll-free: Phone 888-378-2537 6:30AM – 3PM PST; Fax 888-481-2665

Back Issues: Please send me the following issues at $29 each
(Important: please include series initials and issue number, such as HE114.)

_____

_____

_____

$ _____   Total for single issues

$ _____   SHIPPING CHARGES: SURFACE   Domestic   Canadian
                                     First Item $5.00 $6.00
                                     Each Add'l Item $3.00 $1.50
               For next-day and second-day delivery rates, call the number listed above.

Subscriptions: Please __start __renew my subscription to *New Directions for Higher Education* for the year 2_____at the following rate:

U.S.	__Individual $80	__Institutional $180
Canada	__Individual $80	__Institutional $220
All Others	__Individual $104	__Institutional $254

**For more information about online subscriptions visit
www.interscience.wiley.com**

$ _____   Total single issues and subscriptions (Add appropriate sales tax for your state for single issue orders. No sales tax for U.S. subscriptions. Canadian residents, add GST for subscriptions and single issues.)

__Payment enclosed (U.S. check or money order only)
__VISA __MC __AmEx #_____ Exp. Date _____

Signature _____ Day Phone _____
__ Bill me (U.S. institutional orders only. Purchase order required.)

Purchase order # _____
                 Federal Tax ID13559302   GST 89102 8052

Name _____

Address _____

_____

Phone _____ E-mail _____

For more information about Jossey-Bass, visit our Web site at www.josseybass.com

NEW DIRECTIONS FOR HIGHER EDUCATION
IS NOW AVAILABLE ONLINE AT WILEY INTERSCIENCE

What is Wiley InterScience?

Wiley InterScience is the dynamic online content service from John Wiley & Sons delivering the full text of over 300 leading scientific, technical, medical, and professional journals, plus major reference works, the acclaimed *Current Protocols* laboratory manuals, and even the full text of select Wiley print books online.

What are some special features of Wiley InterScience?

Wiley InterScience Alerts is a service that delivers table of contents via e-mail for any journal available on Wiley InterScience as soon as a new issue is published online.
Early View is Wiley's exclusive service presenting individual articles online as soon as they are ready, even before the release of the compiled print issue. These articles are complete, peer-reviewed, and citable.
CrossRef is the innovative multi-publisher reference linking system enabling readers to move seamlessly from a reference in a journal article to the cited publication, typically located on a different server and published by a different publisher.

How can I access Wiley InterScience?

Visit http://www.interscience.wiley.com

Guest Users can browse Wiley InterScience for unrestricted access to journal Tables of Contents and Article Abstracts, or use the powerful search engine.
Registered Users are provided with a *Personal Home Page* to store and manage customized alerts, searches, and links to favorite journals and articles. Additionally, Registered Users can view free Online Sample Issues and preview selected material from major reference works.
Licensed Customers are entitled to access full-text journal articles in PDF, with select journals also offering full-text HTML.

How do I become an Authorized User?

Authorized Users are individuals authorized by a paying Customer to have access to the journals in Wiley InterScience. For example, a university that subscribes to Wiley journals is considered to be the Customer. Faculty, staff and students authorized by the university to have access to those journals in Wiley InterScience are Authorized Users. Users should contact their Library for information on which Wiley journals they have access to in Wiley InterScience.

ASK YOUR INSTITUTION ABOUT WILEY INTERSCIENCE TODAY!